EX LIBRIS

BOOK OF
CHOCOLATES & OTHER
EDIBLE GIFTS

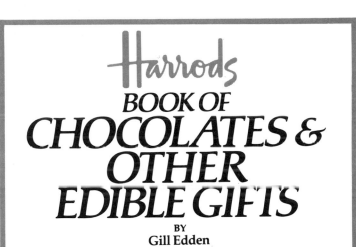

Harrods
BOOK OF
CHOCOLATES &
OTHER
EDIBLE GIFTS

BY
Gill Edden

Grange
BOOKS

Published by Grange Books
An Imprint of Grange Books PLC
The Grange
Grange Yard
London SE1 3AG

This edition published 1994

ISBN 1 85627 579 5

First published by Ebury Press
Random House
20 Vauxhall Bridge Road
London SW1V 2SA

First Impression 1986

EDITORS: Fiona MacIntyre and Barbara Croxford
ART DIRECTOR: Frank Phillips
DESIGNERS: Marshall Art
PHOTOGRAPHY: Grant Symon
STYLIST: Sue Russell
HOME ECONOMISTS: Susanna Tee, Janet Smith and Maxine Clark

Ebury Press would like to thank Harrods, and their archivist
Margaret Baber, for allowing the use of the black and white
illustrations taken from Harrods catalogues.

Computerset by MFK Typesetting Ltd, Hitchin, Herts
Printed and bound in Italy by New Interlitho Spa, Milan

Contents

*All eggs used in this book are size 2
unless otherwise stated.*

Introduction

THE CONFECTIONER'S art is a frivolous pastime, deemed unnecessary in the serious world. Who, after all, needs to eat sweets? But the fun of making them and the luxury of the results are their own reward.

Home-made chocolates, sweets and petits fours will figure as a treat in any household, as much pleasure for the cook to create as for everyone to eat. And as an inexpensive, thoughtful gift, they must come top of the list.

It is an age-old custom to offer small gifts of food on special occasions. For birthdays, anniversaries and religious festivals such gifts are traditional. In some cases, even the form of the food required is traditional, such as the chocolate Easter egg in Britain or spiced Christmas biscuits in Germany. There are other times, too, when a small gift is deemed appropriate, particularly when you are accepting hospitality. On such occasions as these, home-made chocolates, sweets or petits fours draw a pleasing balance between a gift that is merely a token gesture and one that comes with genuine care and affection.

Most people's first experience of sweet-making comes in childhood, as an entertainment on a wet afternoon. At that stage, the choice will usually be of uncooked sweets that can be made simply, and without danger, by young inexperienced hands. These are a good introduction to the art, and will whet the appetite for more adventurous forays.

But as soon as you venture into the realms of boiled sugar, the task becomes more demanding. It requires patience, precision and a certain degree of dexterity. But still the fun remains – and even first attempts, which may not be as confidently executed and perfectly shaped as you might like, will give pleasure in the making and consumption.

After uncooked sweets, the next most common step is to fudges. The techniques of fudge-making are relatively forgiving; there are a variety of possible results, all of which are acceptable. If one member of the family likes a creamy fudge, another will like it crisp and candyish, so nothing can actually be considered 'wrong'. Shaping is easy and the sweet keeps quite well. As a gift, you can even pack fudge and send it by post successfully. Fudge, therefore, provides a good confidence builder for the beginner in boiled sugar sweet-making.

For the family cook, toffees and boiled sweets yield enormous fun. Traditional molasses toffee, old fashioned humbugs, barley sugar sticks and fruit drops all appeal to children. The varied colours and shapes have an element of fantasy that are as important as their flavours. However, they are quite difficult to make. The high sugar temperatures required are dangerous with youngsters around, the syrup burns easily and handling techniques require practice before they can be totally successful. But the processes are fascinating, and pulled and twisted sweets add another dimension to the confectioner's art.

Probably the most useful technique to master is that of fondant making. With a single batch of fondant, you can create both glistening fondant shapes and creamy centres for chocolates. You can even use fondant for icing cakes. It keeps well, too. You can make a large batch of the basic mixture to keep for several weeks and use for different purposes. Experiment to your heart's content with new flavours and delicate colours.

But of all types of confectionery, chocolates shine through, with the most impressive looking results for the least effort. The basic product comes to you ready made, and dipping, coating or moulding are not difficult. Only the centres require imagination. The results, even for a beginner, are pure luxury.

Many preserves make popular edible gifts, but none are more luxurious than candied or glacé fruits. Candying is an attractive way of using seasonal fruits when there is a glut. They keep well, so there is no need to worry about finding a suitable recipient immediately. Candied fruits make an unusual standby gift to keep in your store cupboard – so long as you do not let the rest of the family know they are there, because if you do they will certainly disappear! Each type of fruit is best candied separately so take your time and prepare each kind in turn, ready to make up mixed boxes when gift time comes.

Petits fours are a more spur of the moment 'make today, give tonight' gift. They make a perfect present to take with you to a dinner party, though it may be as well to tell your host or hostess first. Petits fours will always round off a party meal perfectly. The guests may think they have eaten well already, but a tempting sweet morsel served with the after dinner coffee is rarely refused. A tempting box of truffles or a gift wrapped plate of mixed plain and fancy petits fours is a pretty compliment to any cook.

◆ MEASURING ◆

Spoon measures are level. Standard British measuring spoons have been used in testing the recipes throughout this book.

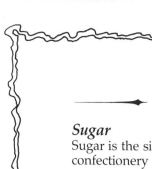 
→ INGREDIENTS ←

Sugar

Sugar is the single most important ingredient in confectionery – without it, few sweets would exist. Granulated sugar is used for most recipes where the mixture is heated, but different types of brown sugar can be used in toffee and fudge recipes to vary the flavour. Caster sugar can be used instead of granulated if you wish; it dissolves a little more quickly but otherwise will give no different results. Lump sugar likewise will make no difference to the finished sweet, but will cost you a little more. In uncooked recipes, you need to use fine, powdered icing sugar to produce a smooth texture.

Other sweeteners, such as honey, golden syrup or glucose, and acids such as vinegar, cream of tartar or lemon juice, are all used to control the re-crystallisation of the melted sugar as it cools; the ingredient used depends on the recipe. Honey and golden syrup affect flavour as well, whereas the other additions affect only the size of the new crystals that form in the sugar as it cools. The quantity of these crystal 'inhibitors' used in any recipe is crucial – alterations from the basic proportion will give a sweet of a very different texture.

Flavourings

Modern cooks have an advantage over old-fashioned sweet makers in the wide range of bottled essences and flavouring oils available. Without them, the distillation of concentrated flavourings, such as fruit juice, would be a long and time-consuming process. Just a few drops, or perhaps 2.5 ml (½ tsp), of these essences is enough to shine through the sweetness of the sugar without altering the texture of the basic mixture.

But do buy good-quality products. Generally, a label that proclaims 'essence of' or 'oil of' means the real product, whereas 'flavouring' is likely to be a synthetic substitute. The difference is quite marked in use.

Colourings

Use colourings sparingly or you will have garish results. If a recipe says 'a few drops', it means maybe three or four drops, not a splash. Some bottles are fitted with dropper tops; otherwise dip a skewer into the bottle and shake the drops off the end of the skewer to control the amount you use. Never tip the bottle up over the sweet mixture, in case you slip!

Fruit and nuts

It always pays to buy top-quality dried fruits. The flavours are much better than cheaper brands and the difference is noticeable in the finished sweets. Nuts are best bought in the shell as these have maximum moisture and flavour. Next best are shelled but with the skins left on. Nuts which have been skinned, or worse still chopped or ground, before packing have too much surface exposed to the air; they will have dried out and lost a considerable amount of their flavour. Buy nuts in small quantities as and when you need them. The longer they sit in your cupboard, the more flavour they lose. Processors, packers and distributors are more likely to have suitable storage conditions than you are.

You will find that many of the recipes in

this book suggest toasting nuts. This intensifies the flavour so that it stands up better against the all-intrusive sweetness of such mixtures as fondant or fudge.

Chocolate

Almost any kind of chocolate can be used for home-made confectionery, depending on your personal preferences and on what is available in your area. A product labelled 'cooking chocolate' will usually be easier to use for dipping, coating and moulding than ordinary eating chocolate. This is usually sold broken into rough chunks and packed simply in polythene bags. It contains a higher proportion of vegetable fat than eating or dessert chocolate, which helps it flow more freely when melted. Chocolate chips and dots sold for baking are similar.

When using a dessert chocolate for coating and moulding, add a little pure vegetable fat to thin it down and achieve a better coating consistency. The flavour of dessert chocolate is generally better than cooking chocolate, so I tend to use dessert types for fillings and cooking chocolate for the outer coating. Whatever happens, never use chocolate-flavoured cake covering for confectionery – it does not set well enough and has a poor flavour.

Plain chocolate tends to be easier to use than milk, possibly because of the presence of extra animal fat in the paler version. But white chocolate can be used quite successfully. A selection of mixed plain, milk and white chocolates looks attractive, but in practice most people seem to prefer to eat the plain, dark version: it is better therefore to choose plain chocolate if you are ever undecided.

◆ EQUIPMENT ◆

Very little special equipment is needed for making chocolates and sweets. A good, heavy saucepan and a wooden spoon are the most important items. A thermometer is the only piece of equipment I would recommend you buy especially for your first attempt at confectionery making. And you can even do without this, if you use the tried and tested cold water tests listed on page 15; however, they are less reliable than a thermometer until you have long experience of sugar boiling.

Saucepans

Use a heavy saucepan, always choosing one larger than the initial quantity of ingredients would seem to warrant. Most of the recipes involving boiling sugar in this book were made in 2.8 or 4 litre (5 or 7 pint) saucepans. Aluminium is the best material to use as it gives the most even heat distribution. Stainless steel is satisfactory so long as the base of the pan has a heavy aluminium or copper core, but there is a tendency for syrup at the sides of the pan to scorch so constant attention is required.

Enamelled saucepans are not suitable, as the heat of boiling sugar may damage the surface.

Non-stick coatings on pans are equally fragile. In theory, an uncoated cast iron pan should be ideal, but in practice I find that the cast iron gets too hot too quickly, and the pan retains its heat too long after you remove it from the stove, making it almost impossible not to scorch the syrup. Use tin-lined copper pans if you are lucky enough to own them.

To clean a toffee-coated saucepan, do not struggle with harsh cleaners and wire wool. Simply fill the saucepan with fresh water and simmer until all the sugar has dissolved.

Thermometer

For sugar-boiling, the temperatures required range between about 200° and 350°, but the most useful thermometer is a multi-purpose candy thermometer graduated from 50° right up to 500° or more. You can use this for many cooking processes – from yogurt-making, through fruit canning and jam-making and on to deep fat frying. It should have a moveable clip to fasten it to the side of the saucepan. Choose a thermometer that has the bottom of the bulb protected, so that it does not come into direct contact with the pan base.

Do not put the thermometer in the syrup until all the sugar has dissolved, or you will risk grains of sugar clinging to the thermometer. Never plunge it straight into boiling syrup either or it may break – leave the thermometer standing in a jug of hot water to warm up until required. Equally do not take it out of boiling syrup and put it directly onto a cold surface or into cool water; a jug of boiling water will both protect the thermometer from the possible damage caused by a sudden temperature change and soak off the sticky sugar.

To take an accurate reading on a thermometer, always bend down and read it at eye level, taking care to be far enough away to protect your face from any spitting syrup. One or two degrees above or below the specified temperature will affect the finished candy, and the distortion caused by reading the thermometer from above is enough to spoil a batch of fondant or fudge.

Spoons and spatulas

Use a wooden spoon for stirring, so that the handle does not get hot, but have a metal spoon handy to check that the sugar has dissolved before you start to boil. Any residual grains of sugar in a syrup will be clearly visible on the surface of a metal spoon, though totally invisible on wood. Use a strong wooden spatula for working fondant.

Heat diffuser

Unless you are particularly lucky with the simmer controls on your stove, you will find a heat diffuser invaluable for achieving the low, even heat required for melting chocolate and fondant. These usually take the form of a double mat of pierced metal, with a handle for easy lifting.

left WALNUT CUPS (page 36); bottom CHOCOLATE HAZELNUT CLUSTERS (page 24); right SOFT ALMOND CENTRES (page 27)

Baking sheets

Marble is the traditional surface for cooling and working fondant and toffee. But few people have a large marble slab in the kitchen these days, and for large quantities you need retaining sides anyway. I use large enamelled baking sheets, but they must be scrupulously clean. If the sheets have any traces of ancient baking on them, soak thoroughly first in washing soda and boiling water or clean with an oven cleaner.

Tins

For most fudges and toffees, you need shallow square or oblong baking tins; foil dishes can be substituted for these. Oil them well before use to make turning out easier. The size most commonly used in this book is an 18 cm (7 inch) square tin.

Moulds

Moulds for fondants and chocolates come in rubber or plastic sheets, flexible for easy turning out. Easter egg moulds are also made of flexible plastic. They are readily available from cookware shops, department stores and suppliers of plastic freezer and microwave ware. But the easiest moulds for chocolate are foil or paper sweet cases that can be peeled off when the fragile shell is set, making pretty chocolate cups.

Cutters

You do not need a great range of fancy cutters, but one or two shapes of the right size will be useful. Cutters about 2–2.5 cm (¾–1 inch) in diameter are the most suitable. Look out for them in specialist cookware shops. If you do not have cutters the correct size, use a sharp knife and make square, diamond and oblong shapes which are just as effective.

Dipping ring and fork

A dipping ring is a small wire hoop with a wooden handle, used to hold the centres while you dip them in chocolate or fondant. A dipping fork is similar but open ended – I find the ring easier to use. Dipping rings and forks are easy enough to obtain in cookware shops but for occasional use or if you cannot obtain them substitute the wrong end of a skewer.

Rubber gloves

Professionals use their bare hands but, for a beginner, rubber gloves are the ideal protection when handling hot fondant or toffee.

Pan stand

Saucepans containing boiling sugar become exceptionally hot. Protect your work surfaces with a pan stand.

Paper

Baking parchment, with a slightly waxed finish, is the best surface for drying most sweets and for packing between layers of sweets in a box. Greaseproof paper can be used if that is all you have to hand.

TECHNIQUES

Sugar boiling

The techniques of sugar boiling are fundamental to the art of the confectioner. If the basic syrup is wrong, no amount of shaping and decorating can disguise it.

Start by choosing a mild, dry day for sweet making. Heat or cold, or a damp or humid atmosphere will all spoil the results. Toffees will be sticky and fondants will refuse to set.

Using a heavy saucepan, of a size that allows plenty of room for the boiling sugar to rise in the pan, dissolve the sugar slowly over a gentle heat. Stir the mixture all the time as the sugar dissolves and do not allow it to come to the boil while there are still crystals present. If necessary at this stage, you can move the saucepan on and off the heat to prevent it boiling, but it is preferable to use a heat diffuser. Stir with a wooden spoon so that you can leave the spoon in the pan without the handle becoming hot, but when you think the sugar is dissolved, check with a metal spoon. Scrape the bottom of the pan and go well into the corners to check that there are no crystals remaining. If there are any crystals left, they will show clearly on the metal spoon.

Once the sugar is dissolved, put in the thermometer, clipping it to the side of the pan, and turn up the heat. The sugar should boil fairly fast to the required temperature but avoid turning the heat too high at first or the syrup may burn. A steady, moderate heat is better than a fluctuating one. Do not stir once the sugar has boiled unless the recipe specifically says that you should – stirring will cause the sugar to re-crystallise, which in most cases will spoil the finished sweets.

Recipes that include milk, cream or butter may need stirring occasionally as the milk solids are liable to burn on the base of the pan unless disturbed from time to time. Draw the wooden spoon carefully across the base of the pan and if there are no signs of sticking, leave it alone.

From time to time while the sugar is dissolving and boiling, brush round the sides of the saucepan with a pastry brush dipped in water. This will dissolve any grains of sugar that form on the sides of the pan above the general level of the syrup – these too could spoil the whole batch if allowed to remain. Professional confectioners achieve the same result by putting a lid on the pan, so that steam condenses and runs down the sides of the saucepan. (I prefer to be able to see what I am doing.)

The sugar-boiling process requires extreme patience. It often takes a good hour for the quantities used in this book to reach the required temperature. And you cannot go away and leave the pan, as you would with a simmering stew or stock, because boiling sugar rises so readily in the pan and may quickly boil over. The temperature is extremely high and the hot spilled syrup is dangerous – as dangerous as boiling fat. Watch the thermometer closely as the correct temperature approaches and if it is rising very quickly, lower the heat to control the rise, or it may boil over the top even as you watch.

As soon as the thermometer registers the correct temperature, remove the pan from the heat. Do not just turn off the heat source – the hob itself will still be hot and may continue to push up the temperature. Take the saucepan off the hob and place it on a pan stand until the bubbles have subsided. Some people like to dip the base of the pan in cold water to cool it more quickly. As soon as the bubbles subside, pour the syrup into the tin, or follow the recipe instructions.

How you handle the sugar when it comes off the heat has as much effect on the finished sweets as how you handle it during boiling. A mixture that is stirred or beaten while still very hot will quickly grain, or re-crystallise, and if you are not careful may well set before you can turn it out of the pan. This is how you achieve a crisp, candyish fudge, for example.

So, for a clear, shining toffee or boiled sweet, do not stir at all after boiling. Simply pour the hot syrup into the prepared tin. For a sweet that is to be opaque but still smooth textured, stir lightly. Leaving the mixture to cool somewhat before stirring lessens the effect and gives you more control; try this if you like a smooth, creamy fudge, not too grainy. For many fudges, the stirring that is necessary during boiling, to stop the milk solids burning, is sufficient in itself and once the mixture has cooled slightly you can pour it straight into the tin.

'Pulling' is another method of changing the appearance of boiled sugar. Many toffees and boiled sweet mixtures are first poured on to a cold tin, while still hot, and left until cool enough to handle. Then, when set firmly enough to be picked up in a sheet, you start to work the mixture with your hands. Fold the sheet of sugar sides to middle and pull it out, fold again and pull again. The more you fold, twist and pull, so the toffee turns from clear to opaque and silky looking and it gradually sets.

Fondant also depends on the method of working it after boiling to the correct temperature. For fondant, the mixture is tipped on to a cold surface and worked with a spatula until it becomes hard and crystalline. You then use the warmth of your hands to knead it to a smooth, fine texture.

The addition of glucose, honey, golden syrup, cream of tartar, vinegar or lemon juice to the basic syrup all contribute to regulating the size of the crystals in the finished sweets.

Cold water tests

Never, ever, touch boiling sugar without first dropping it into cold water. None of the tests is totally accurate, but with experience you will be able to judge the temperature of the sugar from its appearance. Even if you have a thermometer, it is worth doing the tests from time to time, in case you drop and break the thermometer in the

middle of a batch of sweets! Take the saucepan off the heat while testing. The names given to the various stages very slightly from cook to cook.

Thread 102–104°C (215–220°F). Dip two small spoons in cold water then quickly in and out of the syrup. The backs of the spoons will slide easily over each other, but a thread of syrup will form between them. This is a thin syrup suitable for fruit salads or for thinning fondant.

Soft ball 113–118°C (235–245°F). Spoon a little syrup into a bowl of cold water. Leave it for a moment to cool then remove and roll the syrup between your fingers into a ball. At 113°C (235°F) the ball will be very soft and will flatten when you first take it out of the water. The higher the temperature, the firmer the ball becomes. This is the range of temperatures for fudge and fondant.

Hard ball 118–130°C (245–265°F). Spoon a little syrup into cold water, then roll into a ball. The ball should be quite firm but not rock hard. Caramels, nougat and marshmallows are boiled to these temperatures.

Small crack 132–143°C (270–290°F). Spoon a little syrup into cold water. It should separate into small, hard pieces but should not be brittle. Use this range for toffees and some boiled sweets.

Hard crack 149–154°C (300–310°F). Spoon a little syrup into cold water. It will separate into hard, brittle threads. At 154°C (310°F) the syrup will be starting to turn a light golden colour. This high temperature is used for really hard toffees.

Caramel 160–162°C (320–325°F). The syrup will be a rich golden colour. At this stage it is used for praline and for brittle caramel decorations.

Beyond this temperature, the syrup gradually turns a very dark brown and then black, the sweetness goes and it acquires a burned flavour.

This type of syrup is not used for confectionery, but is a colouring for gravies and dark fruit cakes.

◆ STORAGE ◆

Most home-made sweets are best eaten fairly quickly after making; uncooked sweets should be eaten within a few days. Certainly, sugar is a superb preservative, and there is little danger to health in eating cooked sweets that have been made some time. But the appearance and general condition, even of cooked sweets, does deteriorate quite quickly. Commercial confectionery has preservatives and stabilisers added.

As far as possible, store sweets in airtight containers. If you are giving them away as presents in non-airtight packages, leave the decorative packing until the last reasonable moment. Store different types of confectionery separately, to prevent cross-flavouring.

In particular, sweets are affected by temperature and humidity. Toffee left in a cold place will go sticky very quickly, and one piece will irretrievably glue itself to the rest. Chocolate goes grey and dry looking in the cold, losing that lovely glossy bloom that makes it so attractive. Heat will melt chocolate, and start sugar running; 12–18°C (55–65°F) seems to be the median.

Most sweets are best separated from each other, either by individual sweet cases, by wrapping paper or by layers of baking parchment or waxed paper. Wrap toffees, caramels and boiled sweets individually in cling film, foil or cellophane. Pack chocolates and softer sweets flat in boxes, not more than two layers deep, with card or parchment between the layers. This prevents them sticking to each other and the shapes

from distorting. Fudge is one of the best-tempered sweets in storage. It will emerge in good condition several weeks later, not quite so perfect as when it first went in, but certainly in better condition than any toffee or chocolate stored for the same length of time. Fondant keeps relatively well too, though losing the pristine, glittery finish it has when freshly made.

The only sweets that are best not eaten immediately are caramels. These are best left for two to three days, perhaps up to a week, to mature. By then, a very soft caramel will have hardened up a little, harder ones will have become pleasantly chewy. Candied and glacé fruits keep for several weeks without noticeable deterioration too, if packed in flat layers between sheets of parchment.

➤ PACKING EDIBLE GIFTS ➤

All foods should be wrapped or properly stored as soon as they are made, to keep them in good condition. But leave gift wrappings until the last minute, so that they are absolutely fresh for the occasion. Certainly it is worth taking a little trouble with packaging because it can make all the difference to the finished result. If you think your sweets look a little amateurish just wait until you have packed them up! Choose a pretty gift box, line it carefully and put the sweets in individual sweet cases before you pack them and, hey presto, they will become the most sophisticated of gifts.

Individual wraps
Good packaging materials specially designed for confectionery are hard to find. Without doubt,

dark brown waxed paper cases and sheets of dark brown waxed paper are the most enhancing, so do search in specialist shops. The sheets of brown waxed paper are particularly elusive, so if you do track some down, buy a good stock. Plain bright colours also look good, especially if you use a different colour for each type of sweet in a selection. The least attractive are those most readily available – white waxed cases with a floral design – but even these have their uses. Also available are coloured foil cases, particularly pretty for chocolates. One or two in a selection add a sparkle to your gift.

It is advisable to buy ready made sweet cases before you make the sweets, to check on sizes. Some are rather small and you may need to choose a different cutter, or otherwise adjust the size of your sweets to fit.

For hard sweets, clingfilm and foil are the best utility wrappings, but these do not look good in a gift box. Hard shiny sweets such as toffee or clear mints look marvellous wrapped in cellophane, either plain or coloured. The stiff, clear film enhances the shine of the sweets and stays looking crisp and fresh. Baking parchment or waxed paper can be wrapped into neat parcels round square or oblong sweets, or you can use the traditional toffee wrap, twisting the paper in opposite directions at each end. Be sure to cut each square of paper or cellophane large enough; you need about twice the length of the sweet.

Ordinary baking parchment or waxed paper is rather plain and you may like to overwrap it with a strip of coloured foil. This foil can be bought either as specially cut sweet wrappers or in a large sheet, as gift wrapping paper. The former are inclined to be small and you will find it less

restricting to cut your own. Foil wraps can be used underneath cellophane too, for extra colour with the shine.

Petits fours are more difficult to pack than sweets, being on the whole larger and of more variable shape. Small, round petits fours cases are easy enough to find, but long ones (for instance, for éclairs) or slightly larger ones, are more difficult. Overcome this by making your own separators. Take a large sheet of baking parchment or waxed paper and pleat it at intervals to provide a flat base for a row of cakes or pastries, with a wall of paper between each row.

Boxes and other containers

Stationers and department stores sell pretty gift boxes in all sorts of shapes, sizes and colours. These provide the simplest way of packing your gift of sweets, tied with ribbon or gilt thread. If possible, choose shallow boxes that will take a single layer, or at most two layers, of sweets. (Piling up consecutive layers will leave the bottom layer squashed out of shape.) Line the box with dark waxed paper, if possible, or with a plain bright wrapping paper to tone with the outside of the box, or with a doiley – white, gold or silver.

For less delicate sweets, bright miniature carrier bags are a simple idea. Or you can make your own bag from a sheet of gift wrapping paper, choosing a simple envelope shape,

tramp's bundle, cone, Christmas cracker or any other shape or idea your imagination and talents will run to.

A simpler wrap can be made with ordinary kitchen disposables. Shallow foil freezer dishes, paper plates or ovenproof cardboard dishes can all be made to look pretty with a decorative lining and individual sweet cases. Clingfilm makes an effective utility cover, but cellophane looks better, wrapped smoothly over the top and fastened underneath with sticky tape. Tie a ribbon round or fasten a self adhesive bow on top to finish off the gift.

Reusable containers make popular gift wrappings. A glass storage jar or painted tin may well cost you no more than a one-use gift box. It has the advantage of being airtight, to keep the sweets in good condition for longer, and the recipient will be able to use the container afterwards. A ribbon bow and a gift card are all the trimmings needed.

A more elaborate choice, particularly suited to a gift of petits fours, fondants or chocolates, would be a pretty china plate or glass dish. Less obvious containers might include an individual cup and saucer or mug, a cut glass tumbler or small basket. In each case, the container itself makes the wrapper, with only a transparent film of cellophane and a ribbon needed for the finishing touch.

Chocolates

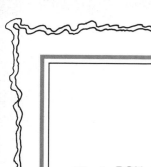

BOX of home-made chocolates is probably the most glamorous of the edible gifts you might give, and yet in many ways chocolates are the easiest sweets to make. You can be endlessly inventive with the centres, or you can use ready-made candied fruit or whole nuts. Whatever you use for centres, the dark glossy coating of chocolate will look inviting and sophisticated.

The easiest chocolate to use for home confectionery work is the type actually sold as 'cooking chocolate'. You will find it in speciality grocers, usually packed in odd-sized pieces in simple polythene bags. It will melt easily to a perfect working consistency. With this type of chocolate, dipping is easy, cups and moulded shapes are strong and crisp. The flavour is only marginally less good than dessert chocolate.

There is also a wide range of plain or milk dessert chocolates. These are all more or less suitable, though plain chocolate is generally easier to work with than milk. Dessert chocolate melts to a running consistency less easily than cooking chocolate, and it helps to add just a little pure vegetable fat to thin it. A really tiny amount is

enough – less than 7 g (¼ oz) vegetable fat will bring 225 g (8 oz) plain chocolate to just the right consistency. Check the pack carefully to make sure that you use *pure* vegetable fat for this purpose – animal fats do not have the same effect. Chocolate dots or chocolate chips, obtainable in most supermarkets, come close to cooking chocolate for workability.

By contrast, the worst you can choose is 'chocolate cake covering'. Apart from tasting poor, this is usually a very soft chocolate that never really sets to a good hard chocolate casing.

You will find that most of the recipes in this chapter use plain or cooking chocolate – plain giving the best flavour, cooking the easiest coating.

The quantity of chocolate needed for any particular purpose will vary with the type of chocolate chosen. So while the various types are interchangeable to suit your own tastes and convenience, the quantities needed will not remain the same. Cooking chocolate goes further than plain dessert chocolate; milk chocolate goes less far than either.

To melt chocolate, break it into a bowl and place over a saucepan of hot water. The bowl

CHOCOLATE WALNUT CREAMS (page 26)

should not touch the water, and the water should not be allowed to boil – that way there is less danger of overheating the chocolate. Heat slowly and gently, stirring from time to time until it reaches a good coating consistency. Remove the saucepan from the heat and leave the bowl over the hot water to maintain the temperature. If you have a lot of work to do and the chocolate starts to cool and thicken again, just reheat carefully. The most important point is not to overheat the chocolate or the texture of the coating will be spoiled. About 29°C (85°F) is the right temperature; a thermometer is not really necessary – judging by eye is quite satisfactory.

To ensure you achieve a good coating, do not be mean with the chocolate. Use more than you think you will need rather than trying to skimp it, and pick up a generous coating with each centre you dip. Any left over at the end can be saved for cake decorating or for dessert or sauce-making.

For dipping, use a dipping ring or fork to hold the centres. For most shapes, the ring is more satisfactory, giving a firmer nesting place for the centre. If the proper equipment seems to be unavailable in your area, the ring end of a skewer works quite well. After dipping, hold the chocolate over the bowl for a moment to let the excess run off, then wipe underneath the ring with a skewer. Place each chocolate carefully on a sheet of baking parchment or greaseproof paper to dry, giving each one a gentle push to cover the bottom completely. The slightly waxed surface of parchment makes it easier to lift the finished chocolate when it has hardened.

Finally, dry and store your chocolates at a coolish room temperature of 13–18°C (55–65°F). In too cold an atmosphere the chocolate quickly clouds over, losing its bloom and taking on a greyish look; too warm and it will melt again. It helps preserve the good looks if you put the finished chocolates in a box and cover them as soon as they are dry.

When packing chocolates for a gift, look for the dark brown waxed paper sweet cases, or brightly coloured foil ones. These set off the chocolates to best advantage. The really large chocolates won't fit into cases anyway, but they look good displayed in a box lined with a doily. For the most attractive gift, make up a box of mixed centres rather than packing all one kind together.

Chocolate Orange Creams

The home-made candied peel on page 28 is ideal for decorating this traditional soft centre chocolate. If you use bought peel do be careful as the chopped mixed peel usually sold for cake making is very harsh flavoured and quite unsuitable. At a top quality grocers, you can usually find candied peel in large pieces, which tastes quite good. Otherwise leave the chocolates plain or decorate with silver balls.

225 g (8 oz) basic fondant (see page 42)	about 7 g (¼ oz) vegetable fat
3 drops oil of orange orange food colouring	candied orange peel, to decorate
200 g (7 oz) milk chocolate	
	MAKES ABOUT 350 g (12 oz)

Knead the fondant until pliable, gradually working in the oil of orange and a very little colouring, just to tint it a pale orange. Roll out the fondant to about 1 cm (½ inch) thick on a board lightly dusted with icing sugar. Cut out shapes, using the same cutter each time. Leave the fondants to dry on parchment.

When the centres are thoroughly dry, break the chocolate into a bowl and melt it over a pan of hot water. Add a little vegetable fat if necessary to achieve a dipping consistency.

Using a dipping ring, dip the orange creams one at a time in the chocolate to give them a generous coating. Place on parchment. Before the chocolate dries, place a small piece of candied orange peel in the centre of each one. Leave to dry.

Chocolate Ginger Creams

Fondant makes an excellent centre for chocolate. It keeps well, is firm to dip, and is smooth and creamy when you bite.

225 g (8 oz) basic fondant (see page 42)	about 7 g (¼ oz) vegetable fat
7.5 ml (1½ tsp) syrup from a jar of stem ginger	crystallised ginger, to decorate
200 g (7 oz) plain chocolate	
	MAKES ABOUT 350 g (12 oz)

Knead the fondant until pliable, gradually working in the ginger syrup. Roll out the fondant to about 1 cm (½ inch) thick on a board lightly dusted with icing sugar. Cut out shapes, using the same cutter each time. Leave the fondants to dry on parchment.

When the centres are thoroughly dry, break the chocolate into a bowl and melt it over a pan of hot water. Add a little vegetable fat if necessary to achieve a dipping consistency.

Using a dipping ring, dip the ginger creams one at a time in the chocolate to give them a generous coating. Place on parchment. Before the chocolate dries, place a tiny sliver of crystallised ginger in the centre of each one. Leave to dry.

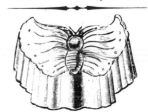

Chocolate Coffee Creams

Different makes of coffee essences vary in their strength of flavour. Add only a few drops of essence to begin with, then taste the fondant and if not strong enough add a little more.

225 g (8 oz) basic fondant (see page 42)
10 ml (2 tsp) double cream
few drops of coffee essence
few drops of brown food colouring

200 g (7 oz) plain chocolate
about 7 g (¼ oz) vegetable fat

MAKES ABOUT 350 g (12 oz)

Knead the fondant until pliable, gradually working in the cream, coffee essence to taste and a little brown colouring if necessary. Roll out the fondant to about 1 cm (½ inch) thick on a board lightly dusted with icing sugar. Cut out shapes, using the same cutter each time. Leave the fondants to dry on parchment.

When the centres are thoroughly dry, break the chocolate into a bowl and melt it over a pan of hot water. Add a little vegetable fat if necessary to achieve a dipping consistency.

Using a dipping ring, dip the coffee creams one at a time in the chocolate to give them a generous coating. Place on parchment. Before the chocolate dries, dip the tip of a skewer in the melted chocolate and lightly trail a line across each chocolate to decorate. Leave to dry.

Chocolate Cherry Creams

Try to keep the decorations on one type of centre all the same – it is a means of identification and looks more professional than random decorating.

225 g (8 oz) basic fondant (see page 42)
10 ml (2 tsp) cherry brandy
200 g (7 oz) plain chocolate

about 7 g (¼ oz) vegetable fat
25 g (1 oz) milk chocolate

MAKES ABOUT 350 g (12 oz)

Knead the fondant until pliable, gradually working in the cherry brandy. Roll out the fondant to about 1 cm (½ inch) thick on a board lightly dusted with icing sugar. Cut into shapes, using the same cutter each time. Leave the fondants to dry on parchment.

When the centres are thoroughly dry, break the chocolate into a bowl and melt it over a pan of hot water. Add a little vegetable fat if necessary to achieve a dipping consistency.

Using a dipping ring, dip the liqueur fondants one at a time in the chocolate to give them a generous coating. Place on parchment. When the chocolate is set, melt the milk chocolate in a bowl over hot water, thinning if necessary with a little vegetable fat. Using the tip of a skewer, decorate the plain chocolates with a squiggle of milk chocolate. Leave to dry again.

CHOCOLATE-DIPPED ORANGE PEEL (page 28)

Chocolate Hazelnut Clusters

These chocolates become favourites with everyone who tries them, and they are simple to make: just add the toasted whole hazelnuts to melted chocolate, then take out four nuts per cluster and leave to dry.

225 g (8 oz) shelled hazelnuts	about 7 g (¼ oz) vegetable fat
225 g (8 oz) plain chocolate	MAKES ABOUT 350 g (12 oz)

Spread the hazelnuts on a baking sheet. Toast in the oven at 180°C (350°F) mark 4 for about 10 minutes, turning them or shaking the tray from time to time. Put the nuts into a clean teatowel and rub off the skins. Leave the nuts to cool.

Break the chocolate into a bowl and melt it over a pan of hot water. Add a little vegetable fat if necessary to achieve a coating consistency.

Remove the pan from the heat, drop in the nuts and stir them round. Using a teaspoon, retrieve four nuts at a time with a good portion of chocolate. Place them in a little heap on parchment. If the chocolate starts to cool and thicken while making the clusters, return the pan to the heat but take care not to overheat the chocolate or it will become too runny to work with. Leave the hazelnut clusters to dry thoroughly.

Chocolate Dipped Fresh Fruit

For these chocolates, choose a fairly firm fruit that does not perish too easily, and one that will not discolour when peeled. Oranges, tangerines and pineapple are ideal, peaches and nectarines are good, and strawberries are delicious if good firm ones are chosen. Do not try to dip raspberries as they will collapse too quickly, and pears or apples are unsuitable as they rapidly turn brown. I have suggested macerating the fruit in Kirsch, but you could choose another liqueur such as Grand Marnier or brandy. These chocolates are best eaten the same day, so they make a good present to take with you to a dinner party. For a more enduring confection, use the same method to dip candied fruit (see page 92).

450 g (1 lb) fresh fruit	about 15 g (½ oz) vegetable fat
60 ml (4 tbsp) Kirsch	
450 g (1 lb) chocolate	

To prepare the fruit, remove any skin or peel. Remove all the pith and membrane from oranges; cut pineapple into rings and then into wedges; cut peaches and nectarines into quarters or slices. Strawberries look pretty with the hulls left in.

Lay the prepared fruit in a shallow dish and spoon the Kirsch over. Leave for 2–3 hours, turning the fruit from time to time. Take the fruit out of the liqueur and dry carefully on absorbent kitchen paper.

Break the chocolate into a bowl and melt it over a pan of hot water. Add a little vegetable fat if necessary to achieve a dipping consistency.

Remove the pan from the heat while you work; keep stirring the chocolate from time to time to keep it evenly melted. If it starts to thicken too much, reheat the water gently until the chocolate is back up to temperature. Put a sheet of parchment beside the pan ready to receive the dipped fruits.

You can either dip the fruit completely in the chocolate, using a dipping fork, or half dip it, holding one end of the fruit in your fingers – it looks pretty and very effective half dipped. Strawberries, even if completely dipped, should be held by the leaves to prevent those becoming coated in chocolate. The surface of the fruit must be completely dry when you dip it, or the moisture will spoil the chocolate. To coat completely, drop a piece of fruit into the chocolate, push it under the surface with a dipping fork then lift out. Hold the coated fruit over the bowl for a moment to drain, then wipe a skewer gently underneath the fork to remove any surplus chocolate. Carefully slide the fruit off the fork on to the parchment. Gently push the fruit very slightly with the fork to seal the chocolate underneath.

Leave until completely dry before removing from the paper, handling them as little as possible.

Dipped Apricot Rounds

To achieve a really dry apricot paste, you must simmer the apricots very slowly – a heat diffuser will help. The result is well worth the trouble as the fruity flavour is delicious.

225 g (8 oz) dried apricots	15 g (½ oz) blanched
50 ml (2 fl oz) water	almonds
50 g (2 oz) granulated	
sugar	MAKES ABOUT 225 g (8 oz)
175 g (6 oz) plain	
chocolate	

Mince or finely chop the apricots and put them in a saucepan with the water. Cover and simmer, stirring, for about 20 minutes until a thick paste forms. Stir in the sugar and simmer, stirring well, for a further 10 minutes until quite dry. Remove from the heat and leave to cool.

When the apricot paste is cold, take a small piece at a time and roll into a ball. Place on parchment and flatten slightly.

Break the chocolate into a bowl and melt it over a pan of hot water. Using a dipping ring, dip the apricot rounds one at a time in the chocolate to give a generous coating. Place on parchment. Before the chocolate dries, decorate each one with an almond. Leave to dry.

Chocolate Walnut Creams

The soft, smooth, nutty paste provides a delightful contrast in texture to the walnut halves. The distinctive shape of the walnut under the chocolate means that no final decoration is needed.

225 g (8 oz) shelled
  walnut halves
100 g (4 oz) caster sugar
½ lightly beaten egg
200 g (7 oz) plain
  chocolate

about 7 g (¼ oz) vegetable
  fat

MAKES ABOUT FORTY

Grind 100 g (4 oz) of the walnuts in a nut mill, blender or food processor. Mix the ground nuts and sugar in a bowl, then work in the egg to form a light paste. Knead the paste with your fingers until firm. Roll out the walnut paste to about 0.5 cm (¼ inch) thick on a board lightly dusted with icing sugar. Cut into circles, using a 2.5 cm (1 inch) plain round cutter. Press a walnut half firmly into each circle of paste.

Break the chocolate into a bowl and melt it over a pan of hot water. Add a little vegetable fat if necessary to achieve a dipping consistency.

Using a dipping ring, dip the walnut rounds one at a time into the chocolate to give them a generous coating. Place on parchment to dry.

Soft Almond Centres

Soft and nutty, these chocolates have an almond paste centre and are decorated with flakes of toasted almonds. Toasting almonds takes only a few minutes yet enhances the flavour enormously.

45 ml (3 tbsp) flaked almonds	about 7 g (¼ oz) vegetable fat
100 g (4 oz) ground almonds	
100 g (4 oz) caster sugar	MAKES ABOUT FORTY
½ lightly beaten egg	
200 g (7 oz) plain chocolate	

Spread the flaked almonds on a baking sheet, toast lightly under a hot grill for a few minutes or in the oven at 180°C (350°F) mark 4 for about 5 minutes. Leave to cool.

Put the ground almonds and sugar in a bowl and work together with a fork, adding just enough egg to bind to a light paste. Knead the paste with your fingers until firm. Roll out the almond paste to about 0.5 cm (¼ inch) thick on a board lightly dusted with icing sugar. With a sharp knife, cut into diamonds 2.5 cm (1 inch) long.

Break the chocolate into a bowl and melt it over a pan of hot water. Add a little vegetable fat if necessary to achieve a dipping consistency.

Using a dipping ring, dip the almond shapes one at a time in the chocolate to give them a generous coating. Place on parchment. Before the chocolate dries, place a flake of toasted almond in the centre of each one.

Chocolate Brazils

Although it adds a little more work, freshly shelled nuts are always better than those you buy ready shelled. Make sure all the brown skin is removed as well as the shell.

200 g (7 oz) plain or milk chocolate	225 g (8 oz) shelled Brazil nuts
about 7 g (¼ oz) vegetable fat	
	MAKES ABOUT 350 g (12 oz)

Break the chocolate into a bowl and melt it over a pan of hot water. Add a little vegetable fat if necessary to achieve a dipping consistency.

Using a dipping ring, dip each nut in turn, rolling it briefly in the chocolate and lifting out quickly. Let the excess chocolate drain off, then place the coated nut on parchment. Leave to dry.

Chocolate-dipped Orange Peel

You can candy orange peel using the method given for fruit on page 92, but the method used in this recipe is much quicker and quite adequate for peel that is not going to be stored for long. Peel candied in this way can be stored for 2–3 months, but for use with chocolate it is nicest used when fresh.

3–4 oranges	225 g (8 oz) plain
granulated sugar	chocolate
½ vanilla pod	about 7 g (¼ oz) vegetable
caster sugar	fat

Scrub the oranges, then carefully remove the peel in quarters. Cut the peel into strips about 0.5 cm (¼ inch) wide. Put the peel in a saucepan, cover with cold water and bring slowly to the boil. Drain off the water, cover with fresh cold water and bring to the boil again. Drain and repeat three more times, then drain and weigh the cooked peel.

Return the peel to the pan and add an equal weight of granulated sugar and the vanilla pod. Just cover with boiling water. Heat gently, stirring, until the sugar has dissolved. Bring to the boil and boil gently until the peel is tender and clear. Remove the pan from the heat and leave to cool.

Remove the peel from the syrup, draining well. Toss in caster sugar. Spread out the pieces on a wire rack and leave to dry. If after several hours it is still sticky, roll in sugar again. Do not store until completely dry.

To coat the peel, break the chocolate into a bowl and melt it over a pan of hot water. Add a little

vegetable fat if necessary to achieve a dipping consistency. With your fingers, break the surplus sugar off the peel.

Using a dipping fork, dip the candied peel, one piece at a time, in the chocolate as for fresh fruit.

Save a few pieces of peel undipped to pack with the chocolate ones – it adds a good colour contrast to the selection in the box.

Noisettes

The centres for these popular chocolates are made from a hazelnut paste, each chocolate being topped with a chocolate coated whole hazelnut.

150 g (5 oz) shelled. hazelnuts	about 7 g (¼ oz) vegetable fat
100 g (4 oz) caster sugar	
½ lightly beaten egg	MAKES ABOUT THIRTY
225 g (8 oz) plain chocolate	

Spread the hazelnuts on a baking sheet. Lightly toast them under a hot grill or in the oven at about 200°C (400°F) mark 6 for 5–10 minutes. Rub the nuts briskly in a teatowel to remove the skins. Grind 100 g (4 oz) of the nuts in a nut mill, blender or food processor, leaving the rest whole.

Mix the sugar with the ground nuts, then work to a paste with the beaten egg. Knead with your fingers until the paste is firm. Roll out to about 1 cm (½ inch) thick on a board lightly dusted with icing sugar. Cut into 2.5 cm (1 inch) squares, using a cutter or sharp knife.

Break a third of the chocolate into a bowl and melt it over a pan of hot water. Add a little vegetable fat

to achieve a good coating consistency. Drop the whole hazelnuts into the melted chocolate and remove them, one at a time, with a dipping ring. Place on parchment and leave to dry.

Break the remaining chocolate into the melted chocolate and melt it over the hot water, adding a little more vegetable fat if necessary to achieve a dipping consistency.

Using a dipping ring, dip the hazelnut paste centres, one at a time, in the chocolate to give them a generous coating. Place on parchment. Before the chocolate dries, put a coated hazelnut in the centre of each one. Leave to dry.

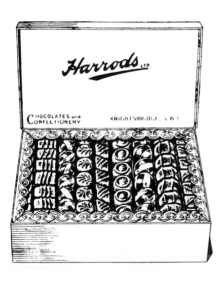

Chocolate Raspberry Creams

Gum arabic is a resin taken from the acacia tree and is used as a setting agent; it is generally obtainable from chemist shops. These mouth-watering raspberry centres are very soft.

350 g (12 oz) icing sugar	225g (8 oz) cooking
15 g (½ oz) gum arabic	chocolate
65 ml (2½ fl oz) cold water	crystallised rose petals
raspberry essence	
red food colouring	MAKES ABOUT FORTY

Sift the icing sugar on to a piece of greaseproof paper. Sprinkle the gum arabic over the water in a small bowl and leave to soak until softened. Place the bowl in a pan of hot water and stir until dissolved. If necessary, strain it through a muslin lined sieve into a larger bowl.

Mix in enough of the sifted icing sugar to form a mixture of piping consistency. Blend in a few drops of raspberry essence and tint very lightly to a pale pink with the red food colouring.

Using a nylon piping bag and 1 cm (½ inch) plain nozzle, pipe small lengths on to parchment. Leave to dry overnight, turning them when it is possible to lift them off the paper.

Break the chocolate into a bowl and melt it over a pan of hot water. Using a dipping fork, dip the raspberry centres, one at a time, into the chocolate to give a generous coating. Place on parchment. Before the chocolate dries, decorate with crystallised rose petals. Leave to set.

Chocolate Mint Crisps

These very smooth chocolate squares or diamonds, studded with tiny pieces of crisp peppermint caramel, are the perfect accompaniments to after-dinner coffee.

50 g (2 oz) granulated
  sugar
50 ml (2 fl oz) water
oil of peppermint
225 g (8 oz) plain
  chocolate
about 7 g (¼ oz) vegetable
  fat

65 ml (2½ fl oz) double
  cream
drinking chocolate
  powder, to dust

MAKES ABOUT 350 g (12 oz)

Oil a baking sheet. Line a small cake tin, about 15 cm (6 inches) square, or a 23×10 cm (9×4 inch) foil dish, with parchment.

Put the sugar and water in a small, heavy saucepan and heat very gently until the sugar has dissolved, stirring continuously. Bring to the boil, without stirring. Add 2–3 drops of oil of peppermint and boil the syrup rapidly to a rich brown caramel. Pour it on to the prepared baking sheet and leave to harden. When the caramel is really hard, crush roughly with a rolling pin.

Break the chocolate into a bowl and melt it over a pan of hot water. Add a little vegetable fat to make it really smooth. Remove from the heat.

Put the cream in a small pan and bring to the boil. Pour on to the melted chocolate and beat until well mixed. Add the crushed peppermint caramel and beat for 2 minutes more, until the chocolate mixture is really smooth and the caramel evenly distributed. Turn the mixture into the prepared tin and smooth the surface. Leave overnight until firm.

Turn out the slab of mint chocolate on to a board and peel off the parchment. Dust a sharp knife with drinking chocolate powder and carefully cut the chocolate mint crisp into square or diamond shapes.

CHOCOLATE MINT CRISPS (above)

Coffee Ganache

Canache is a sort of custard, but is so thick that it sets firmly enough to dip. Because of the cream, these deliciously large chocolates only keep a few days.

1 egg yolk
25 g (1 oz) caster sugar
100 ml (4 fl oz) single
　cream
225 g (8 oz) plain
　chocolate for centres
coffee essence

200 g (7 oz) plain
　chocolate for dipping
about 7 g (¼ oz) vegetable
　fat

MAKES FOURTEEN

Put the egg yolk in a bowl and stir in the sugar until well mixed. Add the cream and blend thoroughly together. Place the bowl over a pan of hot water and cook gently, stirring continuously, until the custard thickens enough to coat the back of a spoon. Remove from the heat and leave to cool.

Break the 225 g (8 oz) chocolate into a bowl and melt it over a pan of hot water. When really soft, remove from the heat and stir in the cooled custard. Add coffee essence to taste. Whisk with a hand-held electric whisk until smooth. Leave to cool until stiff enough to pipe.

Using a nylon piping bag and 1 cm (½ inch) star nozzle, pipe whirls of canache on to parchment, making them about 2.5 cm (1 inch) across. Alternatively, form the custard into egg shapes, using two teaspoons. Put the centres in the refrigerator to harden.

When they are firm enough to handle, break the 200 g (7 oz) chocolate into a bowl and melt it over a pan of hot water. Add a little vegetable fat if necessary to achieve a dipping consistency.

Using a dipping ring, dip the centres one at a time in the chocolate to give them a generous coating. Place on parchment. Leave to dry.

Dipped Orange Ganache

These irresistible orange flavoured set custard centres look especially pretty decorated with home-made candied orange peel (see page 28).

1 egg yolk
25 g (1 oz) caster sugar
100 ml (4 fl oz) single
　cream
225 g (8 oz) plain
　chocolate for dipping
few drops of oil of orange
200 g (7 oz) plain
　chocolate

about 7 g (¼ oz) vegetable
　fat
candied orange peel, to
　decorate

MAKES ABOUT TWENTY FOUR

Put the egg yolk in a bowl and stir in the sugar until well mixed. Add the cream and blend thoroughly together. Place the bowl over a pan of hot water and cook gently, stirring continuously, until the custard thickens enough to coat the back of a spoon. Remove from the heat and leave to cool.

Break the 225 g (8 oz) chocolate into a bowl and melt it over a pan of hot water. When really soft, remove from the heat and stir in the cooled custard. Add oil of orange to taste. Whisk with a hand-held electric whisk until smooth. Leave to cool until stiff enough to pipe.

Using a nylon piping bag and 1 cm (½ inch) star nozzle, pipe the canache into lengths of about 3.5 cm (1¼ inches) on to parchment. Put the centres in the refrigerator to set.

When they are firm enough to handle, break the 200 g (7 oz) chocolate into a bowl and melt it over a pan of hot water. Add a little vegetable fat if necessary to achieve a dipping consistency. Using a dipping fork and holding the centres lengthways, dip them one at a time in the chocolate to give them a generous coating. Place on parchment. Before the chocolate dries, decorate with tiny pieces of candied orange peel. Leave to dry.

Solid Chocolate Eggs

Like all chocolates, these go dull if exposed to the air for long, so wrap them in foil or clingfilm if they are to be kept for more than a day or two before being eaten.

4 eggs	crystallised violets
450 g (1 lb) chocolate	crystallised rose petals

MAKES FOUR

If you have never blown an egg before, now is the time to try. With a needle, pierce a tiny hole in each end of one of the eggs and blow out the contents. Enlarge the hole in one end to take a small piping nozzle and wash out the shell with cold water. Leave to dry thoroughly while you blow the rest of the eggs. (The warmth of a radiator will help with this.) When they are dry, put a piece of sticky tape over the small hole in each egg so that it cannot leak.

Break the chocolate into a bowl and melt it over a pan of hot water, stirring well. When it reaches pouring consistency, spoon into a nylon piping bag fitted with a small nozzle and pipe into the egg shells through the large hole. Swirl it round from time to time to remove any air bubbles. Leave the eggs overnight to set.

Carefully crack the eggs and peel off the shells. Decorate the solid chocolate eggs with crystallised violets, rose petals and narrow ribbons, sticking them on with melted chocolate. Alternatively, wrap each egg tightly in coloured foil. Place them in egg cups or arrange in a basket.

Chocolate Marshmallows

*If you find this marshmallow too difficult to handle, you could increase the quantity of gelatine; but it tastes **much** nicer if only lightly set.*

oil, cornflour and icing
  sugar, for coating tin
275 g (10 oz) granulated
  sugar
about 300 ml (½ pint)
  water
15 g (½ oz) gelatine
5 ml (1 tsp) rose water

red food colouring
1 egg white
drinking chocolate
  powder

MAKES ABOUT 450 g (1 lb)

Oil an 18 cm (7 inch) square baking tin and line the base with greaseproof paper. Oil the paper and dredge with a mixture of a little sifted cornflour and icing sugar.

Put the sugar and 150 ml (¼ pint) water in a heavy saucepan and heat gently, stirring, until the sugar has completely dissolved. Boil steadily to 126°C (260°F), without stirring the syrup.

Meanwhile, sprinkle the gelatine over 45 ml (3 tbsp) water in a heatproof measuring jug and leave to soften a little. Place the jug in a pan of hot water and dissolve the gelatine completely. Make the liquid up to 150 ml (¼ pint) with water and pour into a bowl.

When the syrup reaches 126°C (260°F), pour it on to the dissolved gelatine. Add the rose water and a few drops of red food colouring, then whisk with a hand held electric beater. Add the egg white and continue whisking until the mixture is thick enough to hold its shape. Pour into the prepared tin and smooth the top. Leave to set overnight.

When the marshmallow is set, turn it on to a board dusted with drinking chocolate powder. Cut into 2.5 cm (1 inch) strips, then down into 0.5–1 cm (¼–½ inch) slices. Roll each piece in sifted drinking chocolate powder and arrange in a box, overlapping one piece slightly on the next.

CHOCOLATE EASTER EGG (page 38)

Brandy Cream Cups

For these chocolate cups, foil sweet cases or two paper cases, one inside the other, are the most suitable to use.

250 g (9 oz) cooking chocolate	15 g (½ oz) butter brandy essence
225 g (8 oz) plain chocolate	
100 ml (4 fl oz) double cream	MAKES ABOUT TWENTY FOUR

Break the cooking chocolate into a bowl and melt it over a pan of hot water. Spoon a small amount of the melted chocolate into a foil sweet case or two paper cases, using one inside the other. Swirl the chocolate round until the case is well coated. Leave to dry upside down on parchment. Repeat, making about 24 chocolate cups.

When dry, coat the moulds with a second layer if the first looks thin. Leave to set thoroughly. Keep the remaining chocolate on one side.

Grate the plain chocolate. Put the double cream in a small, heavy saucepan and very slowly bring to the boil. Add the grated chocolate and stir over the heat until melted. Whisk in the butter and brandy essence to taste. Leave to cool.

Spoon a little of the cold brandy cream into each chocolate cup and smooth the tops. Reheat the cooking chocolate until it runs again. Spoon a little chocolate over each cup, smoothing it over and shaking from side to side so that it floods right to the edges. Leave to set.

When the tops are thoroughly dry, peel off the cases and place the chocolate cups in fresh cases.

Walnut Cups

The crunchy, nutty texture provides a pleasing surprise in these chocolate cups. The filling is like a praline but made with walnuts mixed with chocolate.

275 g (10 oz) cooking chocolate	15 ml (1 tbsp) water
50 g (2 oz) shelled walnuts	50 g (2 oz) plain chocolate walnut pieces, to decorate
50 g (2 oz) granulated sugar	MAKES ABOUT THIRTY

Break the cooking chocolate into a bowl and melt it over a pan of hot water. Using foil sweet cases or double paper cases as moulds, spoon a little chocolate into each case and swirl it round to coat. Leave to dry upside down on parchment. Repeat, making about 30 chocolate cups. Apply a second coat if the first one looks thin. Leave to set thoroughly. Keep the remaining chocolate on one side for use later.

Grind the walnuts in a nut mill, blender or food processor. Put the sugar and water in a small, heavy saucepan and heat gently, stirring, until the sugar has completely dissolved. Bring to the boil and boil for 1–2 minutes, without stirring. Remove from the heat, stir in the ground walnuts and set aside.

Break the plain chocolate into a bowl and melt it over a pan of hot water. When the nut mixture and the melted chocolate are about the same temperature, stir them together. Leave to cool before filling the chocolate cups.

Spoon a little of the nut mixture into the chocolate cups and smooth the tops. Reheat the cooking chocolate until it runs again. Flood the top of the cups, covering the filling completely to the edges.

Before the chocolate dries, decorate each one with a small piece of walnut. Leave to set.

When the tops are thoroughly dry, peel off the cases and place the chocolate cups in fresh cases.

Rum and Raisin Cups

There is a superb surprise filling of sponge and raisins soaked in rum when you bite into these chocolates. They make a perfect Christmas gift.

275 g (10 oz) cooking chocolate	120 ml (8 tbsp) rum extra raisins, to decorate
115 g (4½ oz) stale sponge cake	
65 g (2½ oz) raisins	MAKES ABOUT THIRTY

Break the chocolate into a bowl and melt it over a pan of hot water. Using foil sweet cases or double paper cases as moulds, spoon a little chocolate into each case and swirl it round to coat. Leave to dry upside down on parchment. Repeat, making about 30 chocolate cups. Apply a second coat if the first one looks thin. Leave to set thoroughly.

Crumble the sponge and mix in the raisins. Cover with rum and leave until soaked up.

Spoon a little of the soaked cake and raisin mixture into the chocolate cups. Reheat the chocolate until it runs again. Flood the tops of the cups, covering the filling completely to the edges. Before the chocolate dries, place an unsoaked raisin in the centre of each one. Leave to set.

When the tops are thoroughly dry, peel off the cases and place the chocolate cups in fresh cases.

Chocolate Praline

The crunchy praline chocolate centres make a good contrast to the smooth chocolate coating. Crystallised violets make pretty decorations, but if you prefer to keep to nuts, top each chocolate with a flake of toasted almond.

75 g (3 oz) unblanched almonds	200 g (7 oz) cooking chocolate
75 g (3 oz) caster sugar	crystallised violets, to decorate
200 g (7 oz) plain chocolate	
	MAKES ABOUT 450 g (1 lb)

Oil a baking sheet. Put the almonds and sugar in a small, heavy saucepan and heat very gently until the sugar has dissolved, stirring to prevent the sugar sticking to the pan. Continue to heat until the sugar caramelises to a light golden colour and the nuts are lightly toasted. Pour the mixture on to the prepared baking sheet and leave to set. When completely hard, finely crush the praline with a rolling pin or grind in a nut mill.

Break the plain chocolate into a bowl and melt it over a pan of hot water. Mix in the praline to make a stiff paste and turn it into an 18 cm (7 inch) square tin. Leave to set.

Cut the chocolate praline into squares. Break the cooking chocolate into a bowl and melt it over a pan of hot water. Using a dipping ring, dip the chocolate praline, one piece at a time, into the chocolate to give a generous coating. Before the coating dries, decorate each square with a piece of crystallised violet. Leave to dry.

Chocolate Easter Egg

Buy a mould for a hollow chocolate shell from cookware shops or by mail from manufacturers of specialist plastic goods for food – those who make products for the freezer and microwave usually also make moulds suitable for chocolate work. The amount of chocolate to use is not given as sizes of different manufacturer's moulds vary.

Break the chocolate into a bowl and melt it over a pan of hot water. Make sure the bowl does not touch the water, and that the water does not boil. Heat gently until the chocolate melts, stirring gently from time to time. It is ready to use at about 29°C (85°F), when it should be completely melted but quite thick. Add a little vegetable fat if necessary so that the chocolate runs freely and will coat the mould easily.

Remove the bowl from the heat, so that the chocolate does not continue getting hotter, and pour a little into the mould. Tilt and swirl it round until the whole surface is well coated, adding more chocolate as necessary. Place the mould, open side down, on parchment and leave to dry. When dry, you will be able to see if there are any thin areas. If so, melt some more chocolate and add another layer to the mould.

When the chocolate is thoroughly set, it should start to shrink away from the side of the mould. Ease off the mould, then make the second half of the shell (it is quicker to buy two chocolate egg moulds, of course).

Fill one half of the shell with chocolates or sweets, then fill the top half with crumpled parchment, to prevent them damaging. Stick the halves together either by brushing the join with a little melted chocolate, or by piping a decorative pattern all round the join.

Decorate the egg with marzipan flowers or ornamental Easter chicks, ice a name on or add ready made decorations such as crystallised violets or silk flowers, depending whether you are making for a child or an adult. Stick the decorations on with little dabs of melted chocolate. Tie a ribbon to hold the egg securely together.

VANILLA CREAM FONDANTS (page 44)

Fondants

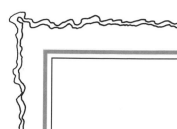

ONDANTS are the epitome of confectionery work. Smooth, sugar morsels, meltingly soft in texture, fine and delicate in flavour, they are also exquisitely pretty to look at. Whether your gift is a box of mixed fondants, or a selection of different types of sweets, the fondants sparkle invitingly, just waiting to be eaten.

Fondant work is somewhat more exacting than other branches of sweet making. Not only is the precise temperature of the boiling syrup important, but so is the working of the syrup into the characteristic, soft texture. The syrup has to be 'turned' with a spatula and then kneaded by hand until fine, even crystals form in a soft and workable mass. The fondant is also best matured for several days before use – it is possible to shape it straight away but much easier and more successful if you wrap the fondant in an airtight package and let it rest. So a gift of fondants is not a spur-of-the-moment affair; a little planning is required to accommodate the different stages.

When making a basic fondant mixture, add some of the sugar in the form of glucose. This will encourage the formation of fine, even-sized crystals instead of large, coarse ones. Then follow the usual rules for sugar boiling (see page 13). Stir the syrup over a very low heat until the sugar has dissolved, without boiling, until there is absolutely no trace of undissolved sugar left. If necessary use a heat diffuser.

Then boil rapidly, without stirring, to the temperature stated in the recipe. If you stir during this boiling, it will encourage the formation of the rough crystals that you do not want.

Have a cold baking sheet or marble slab ready for turning the fondant. Traditionally a marble slab was used, but if you are making more than about 225 g (8 oz) fondant you will need a very large slab indeed to hold the syrup. Also, since boiling sugar syrup is dangerously hot, better be safe than sorry and use a baking sheet with sides about 2.5 cm (1 inch) deep to contain it within bounds. The important factors are that the surface should be really cold and that you should

have room to work – which is why a bowl is not ideal.

There are two basic methods of shaping the final sweets. Either you can re-melt the fondant, flavour and colour it and pour it into moulds. Or you can knead the fondant, roll it out and cut it with fancy cutters. The first method produces a sweet with a slightly finer, smoother texture; use a plastic sheet of moulds, flexible enough to allow you to turn out the finished fondants without damaging them.

To knead and cut the fondant, you need to work in a cool, dry atmosphere. A hot or humid kitchen, even hot lights, makes the fondant too hot to shape. Sometimes even the warmth of your hands will make it too soft by the time you have added liquid flavourings. If this happens, tightly cover the surface of the fondant with clingfilm, then place in the refrigerator overnight to firm up again. Alternatively, sift in a little extra icing sugar. However if the fondant is too hard, knead in a little syrup stock.

At the end of this chapter there are a few recipes for uncooked creams. These are not true fondants, but they are pleasant sweets that are quickly made. Many people will choose to use them for that reason. They are also ideal if children want to be involved in the making – boiling sugar is dangerous with children around. The uncooked creams do not keep well, so should be eaten within two to three days.

Basic Fondant

Traditionally, fondant is worked on a marble slab but for this large quantity that is not really practical, even if you have one. You need a wide baking sheet or tray with deep enough edges to contain the hot syrup; I use the large deep baking sheet supplied with my oven; an alternative might be a large stainless steel mixing bowl.

1.4 kg (3 lb) granulated sugar
50 g (2 oz) powdered glucose

450 ml (¾ pint) water

Put the sugar, glucose and water in a saucepan and dissolve the sugar and glucose slowly over a low heat, stirring all the time. When the sugar is completely dissolved, bring the syrup slowly to the boil. Boil to 115°C (240°F), without stirring. Remove from the heat and leave until all the bubbles have disappeared from the surface.

Sprinkle a little water on a baking sheet and pour the syrup on to it. As the syrup touches the cold, damp surface, it will start to thicken. Leave to cool until a skin starts to form around the edges.

Using a wooden spatula, collect the edges into the centre and work the mixture in a figure of eight movement. It will gradually shrink into a hard, crystalline white lump. Once this is achieved, scrape the fondant off the sheet and knead with your hands until smooth and even textured, soft and pliable.

If possible, the fondant should be left for two to three days before use; in fact, it will keep for up to six weeks if necessary – which is why it is worth making a large quantity at once. Put the fondant in a polythene container with an airtight lid, cover the surface closely with clingfilm and seal the lid on tightly. The clingfilm prevents the surface drying out – if the surface does harden it will spoil the fondant. In hot weather, keep the fondant in the refrigerator.

When you take out part of the fondant for use, be sure to press the clingfilm down over the surface again to keep out the air, and to re-seal the box tightly.

Syrup Stock

Use this syrup to adjust the texture of basic fondant that has hardened during storage. The syrup will keep for four to six weeks.

225 g (8 oz) granulated sugar
150 ml (¼ pint water)

Put the sugar and water in a saucepan and heat gently, stirring until the sugar is dissolved. Bring to the boil and boil without stirring again to 102°C (216°F), a thick syrup. Leave to cool. Strain the cooled syrup through a muslin lined sieve to remove any possible sugar.

left TUTTI FRUTTI CREAMS (page 49);
bottom PEPPERMINT CREAMS (page 49)

Vanilla Cream Fondants

Plain, simple, creamy-flavoured confections, these make a good contrast to a selection of dark chocolates. There are two methods here for shaping the fondant, either in moulds or by rolling out and cutting shapes.

225 g (8 oz) basic fondant
  (see page 42)
10 ml (2 tsp) double
  cream
syrup stock (see page 42)
few drops of vanilla
  essence

Decoration
silver balls
crystallised violets

MAKES ABOUT 225 g (8 oz)

Using fondant moulds

Put the fondant into a bowl over a saucepan of hot water and let it melt. The bowl should not touch the water and the water should not boil.

Stir in the double cream until well blended. If necessary, add a little of the syrup stock – you need only enough syrup to make the fondant pourable, and you may need none at all. When the fondant is of a pouring consistency, remove the bowl from the heat and dry the bottom carefully so that no drops of water drip into the mixture while you are working. Stir in a few drops of vanilla essence.

Carefully spoon or pour the fondant into a sheet of moulds and leave to set and harden. They should be hard enough to turn out in about 4 hours, but they may be better left a little longer before you handle them much.

Gently press two or three silver balls or a crystallised violet into the top of some of them. Place in paper sweet cases.

Shaping with cutters

If you have no moulds, you will have to knead in the cream and flavouring, a little at a time. If the fondant is too hard to handle, add a little syrup; if it is too soft, sift a very little icing sugar over it – no more than 5 ml (1 tsp) – and knead in. Chilling for a while in the refrigerator also helps to make fondant firmer.

When the flavourings are well blended in and the fondant is pliable, roll out to about 1 cm (½ inch) thick on a board lightly dusted with icing sugar. Cut into shapes with a fancy sweet cutter and press the decorations on top straight away. Leave until the outsides have hardened before putting them into paper sweet cases.

Fondants Crème de Menthe

*The crème de menthe gives these fondants a
delicate pale green tint as well as a delicious
minty flavour.*

225 g (8 oz) basic fondant (see page 42)	syrup stock (see page 42)
a little double cream	MAKES 225 g (8 oz)
5–10 ml (1–2 tsp) crème de menthe liqueur	

Melt the fondant in a bowl over a pan of hot water,
as for Vanilla Cream Fondants (see opposite). Stir in
the cream and crème de menthe. If necessary to
make it pourable, add a little syrup stock.

Carefully spoon or pour the mixture into the
fondant moulds and leave to set and harden. Turn
out the fondants and place in paper sweet cases.

Blackcurrant Cream Fondants

*Blackcurrant drink has a good, strong flavour
which is tangy as well as sweet.*

225 g (8 oz) basic fondant (see page 42)	crystallised rose petals, to decorate
5 ml (1 tsp) double cream	
5–10 (1–2 tsp) concentrated blackcurrant drink	MAKES 225 g (8 oz)

Knead the fondant by hand until it starts to soften.
Knead in the cream and blackcurrant flavouring, a
little at a time, to achieve a soft, pliable mixture.

Roll out the fondant on a board lightly dusted
with icing sugar. Cut into shapes to about 1 cm
(½ inch) thick with a fancy sweet cutter and decorate
with crystallised rose petals. Leave to set and
hardened, then place in paper sweet cases.

Alternatively, melt the fondant, add the cream
and flavouring, then pour into moulds as for Vanilla
Cream Fondants (see opposite).

Ginger Fondants

*When the basic fondant is used for coating, it
goes crisp and shiny. Ginger fondants are
delicious – hot-flavoured but sweet, crisp on the
outside, softer in the centre. Use a good-quality
crystallised ginger, not the type sold specifically
for baking which usually has less flavour. Or,
for a really hot confection, try stem ginger,
drying it well before dipping.*

450 g (1 lb) basic fondant (see page 42)	225 g (8 oz) crystallised ginger pieces
syrup from a jar of stem ginger	MAKES ABOUT 450 g (1 lb)

Melt the fondant in a bowl over a pan of hot water.
Thin the fondant with a little syrup from a jar of
stem ginger – it should lightly coat the back of a
wooden spoon.

Using a dipping ring, dip the pieces of ginger one
at a time into the fondant. Lift out, drain for a
moment and place on a wire rack to dry.

Fondants Framboises

Framboise liqueur has a pronounced flavour, producing distinctive raspberry fondants.

225 g (8 oz) basic fondant (see page 42)
10 ml (2 tsp) double cream
1–2 drops pink food colouring

5–10 ml (1–2 tsp) framboise liqueur

MAKES 225 g (8 oz)

Melt the fondant in a bowl over a pan of hot water, as for Vanilla Cream Fondants (see page 44). Stir in the cream. Add pink food colouring to tint the mixture a very pale pink. Remove from the heat and gently stir in the liqueur. Pour into the fondant moulds and leave to set and harden. Turn out the fondants and place in paper sweet cases.

If you are shaping the fondant by rolling out and using cutters (see Vanilla Cream Fondants), you will have to knead in the colouring very thoroughly by hand or it will be streaky.

Baileys Fondants

Irish whiskey-based Baileys liqueur is made with cream, so you do not need any more cream in this recipe.

225 g (8 oz) basic fondant (see page 42)
10 ml (2 tsp) Baileys liqueur

MAKES 225 g (8 oz)

Knead the fondant by hand until it starts to soften. Knead in the liqueur, a little at a time, to achieve a soft, pliable mixture.

Roll out the fondant to about 1 cm (½ inch) thick on a board lightly dusted with icing sugar. Cut into shapes, using a fancy sweet cutter. Leave the fondants to set and harden, then place in paper sweet cases.

Fondant Dates

These popular date sweetmeats, filled with almond-flavoured fondant, are easy to make. Use the almond essence sparingly to avoid a synthetic flavour.

225 g (8 oz) dried dates
225 g (8 oz) basic fondant (see page 42)
1–2 drops almond essence

25 g (1 oz) chopped almonds, toasted
caster sugar, for rolling

MAKES 450 g (1 lb)

Slit the dates lengthwise to remove the stones, leaving the two halves attached.

Knead the fondant until pliable, then knead in the almond essence and chopped nuts until evenly distributed.

Break off a small piece of fondant at a time, roll it into an oval and use to fill the centres of the dates.

Roll the fondant dates in caster sugar. Leave to dry, then place in paper sweet cases.

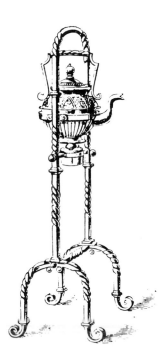

Pistachio Fondants

The nuts in this recipe take the edge off the sweetness – which some people prefer. Pistachio nuts have a green kernel covered by a thin reddish skin and are enclosed in a white shell. Here, the shelled nuts are blanched to reveal the attractive green kernel.

25 g (1 oz) shelled pistachios	few drops of green food colouring
225 g (8 oz) basic fondant (see page 42)	MAKES 225 g (8 oz)
syrup stock (see page 42)	

Blanch the pistachios in a bowl of boiling water for about 10 minutes, then rub off the skins. Chop the nuts finely, reserving a few whole nuts for decoration.

Melt the fondant in a bowl over a pan of hot water, as for Vanilla Cream Fondants (see page 44). Soften if necessary with a little syrup and lightly tint with a few drops of green food colouring. Remove from the heat and stir in the chopped nuts. Pour into the fondant moulds and leave to set and harden.

Turn out the fondants and decorate each one with a halved pistachio. Place in paper sweet cases.

If you prefer to make all the fondants of one flavour in the same shape, you will have to knead in the colouring and nuts, then shape the fondant by rolling out and using a cutter.

Dipped Almond Fondants

The many layers are inclined to make this sweet very large indeed. Keep the inner layer of amaretto fondant as thin as you can.

20 g (¾ oz) blanched almonds	450 g (1 lb) granulated sugar
225 g (8 oz) basic fondant (see page 42)	225 ml (8 fl oz) water syrup stock (see page 42)
7.5 ml (1½ tsp) amaretto liqueur	
	MAKES ABOUT 450 g (1 lb)

Dipping Fondant
tiny pinch of cream of tartar

Prepare the dipping fondant first so that it has a little time to mature before use. Stir the cream of tartar into a little cold water. Put the sugar and water in a saucepan and heat very gently, stirring, until the sugar has completely dissolved. Bring to the boil and add the cream of tartar. Boil to 113°C (236°F) and remove from the heat. This temperature, plus the addition of cream of tartar, will give a slightly softer fondant than the basic mixture.

Let the bubbles subside in the pan, sprinkle a little water on a baking sheet and pour the syrup on to it. Leave to cool until a skin starts to form around the edges. Using a wooden spatula, work the fondant in a figure of eight movement until the sugar crystallises and hardens, then knead by hand until soft and pliable (see page 44). Leave to stand while making the centres.

Spread the almonds on a baking sheet. Toast them lightly under the grill or in the oven at 200°C (400°F) mark 6 for about 10 minutes, shaking and turning them until lightly browned all over. Leave to cool.

Knead the basic fondant, working in the liqueur, until it is soft enough to mould. Break off a small piece at a time and place a toasted almond in the centre. Roll up the fondant round the nut and form into a sphere between the palms of your hands. Leave to dry on parchment until well crusted, turning them so that they harden underneath too.

When the centres are dry, melt the dipping fondant in a bowl over a pan of hot water. Heat gently, stirring all the time, until just below boiling point. Add a little syrup stock if necessary to achieve a dipping consistency. Adjust the heat to keep the fondant at the same temperature, and continue to stir frequently while you work, to prevent a crust forming. Place a sheet of parchment near the pan.

Using a dipping ring, dip the almond centres one at a time into the fondant. Turn over quickly and lift out. Drain for a moment and, as you draw the ring aside, wipe it across the edge of the pan to remove any excess, but without touching the sweet itself. Place the dipped almonds on the parchment to dry. (Remember to keep stirring the dipping fondant as you coat the sweets.)

Leave to dry, then place carefully in paper sweet cases.

Tutti Frutti Creams

Less delicate in texture and flavour than true fondants, these do have the advantage of being quick to make.

90 ml (6 tbsp) double cream
450 g (1 lb) icing sugar
30 ml (2 tbsp) mixed candied peel, very finely chopped
45 ml (3 tbsp) chopped glacé cherries

45 ml (3 tbsp) chopped almonds
juice of ½ lemon
quartered glacé cherries, to decorate

MAKES ABOUT 550 g (1¼ lb)

Put the cream in a large bowl and sift in the icing sugar. Mix with a fork until well blended. Add the chopped peel, cherries, nuts and lemon juice. Knead well by hand until the fondant is smooth and the fruit and nuts well blended in.

Break off small pieces at a time and roll into small balls (dust your hands very lightly with icing sugar if the mixture sticks). Flatten each ball slightly and press a piece of glacé cherry into the top of each one. Place in paper sweet cases and leave to dry.

Peppermint Creams

Add oil of peppermint sparingly as it is very strong! To really control how much you use, dip a skewer into the bottle and shake the drops off the end of the skewer.

1 egg white, size 4
225 g (8 oz) icing sugar
1–2 drops oil of peppermint

MAKES 225 g (8 oz)

Beat the egg white in a bowl until stiff. Sift in the icing sugar and combine well to make a firm mixture. Carefully add the oil of peppermint to taste and blend in thoroughly.

Roll out the peppermint cream to about 0.5 cm (¼ inch) thick on a board lightly dusted with sifted icing sugar. Cut into rounds, using a small round cutter. The trimmings can be kneaded together, rolled out again and used to make more peppermint creams. Leave to dry on a wire rack for about 12 hours. Pack in layers, with waxed paper or parchment between the layers.

Sugar Mice

You can use the basic boiled fondant mixture to make mice by pouring it into a mould – certainly fondant made by the basic method keeps the best and the mice can be stored for some time. But if the children want to help make them, it is safer to avoid boiling sugar and make a simple mixture like this one. It is not as smooth and melty as the boiled one, but will still be very popular.

450 g (1 lb) icing sugar	silver balls
50 g (2 oz) golden syrup	thin white string
1 egg white	
various food colourings	MAKES ABOUT TWENTY FOUR

Sift the sugar into a bowl. Warm the syrup gently until it runs smoothly, then add to the sugar with the egg white. Mix well with a fork then knead by hand to make a smooth mixture.

Divide the mixture into three or four pieces. Leave one portion white and tint the others lightly with pink, yellow or green. Knead colourings in evenly.

Dust a board and your hands with sifted icing sugar and shape the mixture into small mice, no more than about 5 cm (2 inches) long. For each one, make a small sausage shape, pointing it at the nose end. Cut a length of string, tie a knot in the end and press the knot into place under the mouse for a tail. For the ears, make two tiny balls, flatten and curve them and press in place. Use silver balls for eyes. Leave to dry.

Chocolate Creams

These do not have the delicacy of texture of a true fondant, but the flavour is good.

30 ml (2 tbsp) evaporated milk	drinking chocolate powder
225 g (8 oz) icing sugar	toasted almonds, to decorate
10 ml (2 tsp) brandy	
25 g (1 oz) plain chocolate	

MAKES ABOUT 275 g (10 oz)

Put the milk in a bowl and sift in the icing sugar. Using a fork, gradually work together. Add the brandy and knead by hand until well blended.

Melt the chocolate in a small bowl over a pan of hot water. Leave to cool but not thicken. Add the melted chocolate to the brandy flavoured cream, scraping out the bowl well. Knead until the mixture is smooth and pliable.

Roll out the mixture to just over 0.5 cm (¼ inch) thick on a board very lightly dusted with drinking chocolate powder. Cut into rounds, using a small round cutter. Decorate each one with a toasted almond. Leave to dry and harden, then place in paper sweet cases.

SUGAR MICE (left)

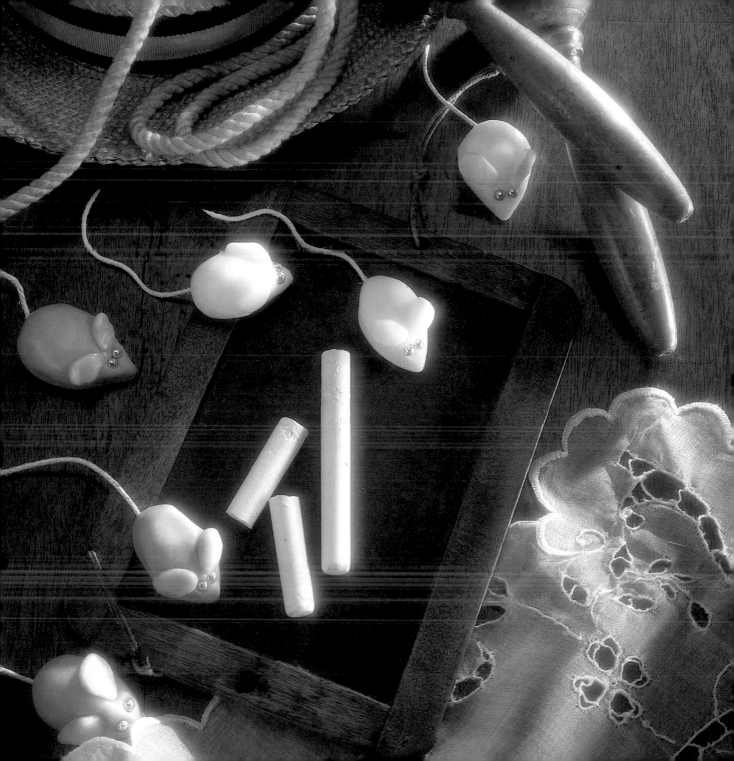

Walnut Coffee Creams

These smooth, creamy, coffee-tasting fondants have a pleasing crunchy texture thanks to the walnut pieces.

30 ml (2 tbsp) evaporated milk	225 g (8 oz) icing sugar
5 ml (1 tsp) Tia Maria liqueur	30 ml (2 tbsp) chopped walnuts
3 drops coffee essence	walnut pieces, to decorate
few drops of brown food colouring	MAKES ABOUT 225 g (8 oz)

Put the evaporated milk, liqueur, coffee essence and colouring in a bowl, then sift in the icing sugar. Mix with a fork until the sugar is incorporated. Add the chopped nuts. Knead by hand until the fondant is smooth and pliable and the nuts are evenly distributed.

Roll out the fondant to about 1 cm (½ inch) thick on a board lightly dusted with icing sugar. Cut into shapes, using sweet cutters. Decorate each one with a piece of walnut. Leave to dry on a wire rack, then place in paper sweet cases.

Clementine Creams

If you don't believe that these will taste any different from orange creams – just try them. The creams are decorated with candied clementine peel.

1 clementine	finely grated rind of 2 clementines
granulated sugar	225 g (8 oz) icing sugar
45 ml (3 tbsp) double cream	orange food colouring
	MAKES ABOUT 225 g (8 oz)

Scrub the whole clementine and remove the peel in quarters. Use water and the granulated sugar to candy the peel, using the method in Chocolate-Dipped Orange Peel on page 28. Leave to dry.

Put the cream and grated rind in a bowl, then sift in the icing sugar. Mix together with a fork. Knead by hand until smooth and pliable. Add a tiny amount of orange food colouring to lightly tint the fondant mixture.

Roll out the mixture to about 1 cm (½ inch) thick on a board lightly dusted with sifted icing sugar. Cut out small shapes, using a fancy sweet cutter.

Cut the candied peel into small diamonds or strips and use to decorate the sweets. Leave to dry on a wire rack, then place in paper sweet cases.

Fudge

UDGE is probably the most popular home-made confectionery. I've never met anyone who didn't like it, and the home-made versions are usually better than mass-produced commercial ones. The finished product always has a slightly rough and ready look about it – you can't make fudge quite so glamorous and glossy as a box of chocolates. But the appeal is similar to that of a steaming hot-pot in an earthenware casserole, compared to smoked salmon on a silver platter. The more homely one has a definite place in everybody's appetite.

Fudge keeps quite well, and the best place for home storage is in an airtight container. When the time comes to give the fudge away, pack it in layers between sheets of waxed paper or baking parchment in a decorative box, or pile it into a glass jar. It is quite good-tempered and the pieces will not stick to each other, so there is no need for individual wrappings. If you are packing the fudge for sale at a bazaar, small polythene bags tied with ribbon are cheap yet pretty.

Fudge is basically a sugar syrup made with milk or cream. Its texture may be soft and creamy or crisp and grainy – tastes vary. I actually prefer the smoother textured fudges, but there are recipes for both kinds in this chapter.

As with all syrups, fudge must be stirred continually until the sugar is dissolved, and must not be allowed to boil until all crystals have disappeared. The point at which this is achieved is less obvious when the liquid is milk or cream as opposed to water, so do watch it carefully. If you stir with a metal spoon, you will be able to see any remaining sugar grains on the spoon. Then, as it boils, stir occasionally to prevent the milk scorching on the base of the pan. If there is butter in the mixture, choose unsalted for preference as it burns less easily.

Adding a little honey or golden syrup makes a softer fudge – it converts some of the sugar to invert sugar which crystallises into fine, even grains instead of large, coarse ones. The other factor which makes a big difference to the texture of fudge is beating it after it has finished boiling. If you beat the mixture while it is still very hot, it will grain quickly and set to a firm, rather granular, fudge. If you let it cool first and do not beat so much, the fudge will be softer and smoother. Try both to see which you prefer.

The usual temperature for making fudge is 115°C (240°F), though you will find small variations on this in some of the recipes producing slightly different fudges.

Vanilla Fudge

This is a smooth, creamy fudge that makes a good base if you want to experiment with flavourings. It is less temperamental than those made with cream.

700 g (1½ lb) granulated
sugar
75 g (3 oz) butter
200 ml (7 fl oz) evaporated
milk

200 ml (7 fl oz) fresh milk
few drops of vanilla
essence

MAKES ABOUT 900 g (2 lb)

Oil an 18 cm (7 inch) square baking tin. Put the sugar, butter and milks into a large, heavy pan and heat gently until the butter has melted and the sugar completely dissolved, stirring continuously. Turn up the heat and boil to 115°C (240°F). Stir the mixture occasionally, to prevent the milk burning on the base of the pan. As the mixture nears the correct temperature, lower the heat a little.

As soon as the temperature reaches 115°C (240°F), remove from the heat and stir in the vanilla essence. Cool a little, then beat just until the mixture starts to leave a trail on itself.

Pour the fudge into the prepared tin. Leave to cool. Before the fudge hardens completely, mark into squares with a sharp knife. When completely cold and set, turn the fudge out and cut carefully into the marked squares.

Ginger Fudge

Make as for Vanilla Fudge, but omit the vanilla essence and beat in 100 g (4 oz) chopped stem ginger as soon as you remove the pan from the heat. Dry as much of the syrup off the ginger as you can, using absorbent kitchen paper, before you chop it. The result is one of the most popular fudges I make – the combination of hot and sweet flavours is a real winner.

VANILLA FUDGE (above); CHOCOLATE AND
HAZELNUT FUDGE (page 57)

Coconut Fudge

Toasting the coconut for this fudge helps to intensify the flavour.

75 ml (5 tbsp) desiccated coconut

700 g (1½ lb) granulated sugar

250 ml (9 fl oz) single cream

30 ml (2 tbsp) golden syrup

3 drops of vanilla essence

MAKES ABOUT 900 g (2 lb)

Oil an 18 cm (7 inch) square tin. Spread the coconut on a baking sheet. Lightly toast under the grill or in the oven at 200°C (400°F) mark 6 for about 5 minutes, shaking it from time to time and watching carefully to make sure the coconut doesn't scorch. Leave to cool.

Put the sugar, cream and golden syrup in a large, heavy saucepan and heat gently until the sugar has dissolved, stirring continuously. Bring to the boil and boil to 115°C (240°F), stirring occasionally.

Remove the pan from the heat, wait for the bubbles to subside and stir in the vanilla essence and coconut. Cool a little, then beat until the mixture starts to leave a trail on itself.

Pour the fudge into the prepared tin. Leave to cool. Mark into squares as it begins to set. When completely cold and set, turn the fudge out and cut into the marked squares.

Coffee and Walnut Fudge

Coffee essences vary. With mild ones, you will need to use about 30 ml (2 tbsp); with stronger varieties you will only need about 5 ml (1 tsp).

700 g (1½ lb) granulated sugar

75 g (3 oz) unsalted butter

200 ml (7 fl oz) evaporated milk (½×400 g (14 oz) can)

200 ml (7 fl oz) fresh milk coffee essence

50 g (2 oz) shelled walnuts, chopped

MAKES ABOUT 900 g (2 lb)

Oil an 18 cm (7 inch) square tin. Put the sugar, butter and milks in a large, heavy saucepan and heat gently until the sugar has dissolved, stirring continuously. Bring to the boil and boil to 115°C (240°F), stirring occasionally, paying particular attention to the base of the pan.

Remove the pan from the heat and beat in the coffee essence and nuts. Cool a little, then beat until the mixture starts to leave a trail on itself.

Pour the fudge into the prepared tin. Leave to cool. Mark into squares as it begins to set. When completely cold and set, turn the fudge out and cut into the marked squares.

Chocolate and Hazelnut Fudge

A delightful creamy, nutty fudge, with a pleasing chocolate flavour.

450 g (1 lb) icing sugar
200 ml (7 fl oz) evaporated milk
25 g (1 oz) butter
175 g (6 oz) plain chocolate, grated

50 g (2 oz) shelled hazelnuts, chopped

MAKES ABOUT 800 g (1¾ lb)

Oil an 18 cm (7 inch) square tin. Sift the icing sugar into a large, heavy saucepan and add the milk and butter. Heat gently until the sugar has dissolved, stirring continuously. Bring to the boil and boil to 115°C (240°F), stirring the mixture occasionally to prevent it sticking and burning on the base of the pan.

Remove the pan from the heat, beat in the chocolate and nuts and continue to beat, if necessary, just until the mixture starts to leave a trail on itself.

Pour the fudge into the prepared tin. Leave to cool. Make into squares as it begins to set. When completely cold and set, turn the fudge out and cut into the marked squares.

Penuche

Penuche is an American-style fudge, with a strong Mexican influence. It is harder than the usual English fudge and darker in colour. Because of the dark colour, take particular care that it is not burning as it boils.

450 g (1 lb) light soft brown sugar
175 ml (6 fl oz) milk
50 g (2 oz) butter

5 ml (1 tsp) vanilla essence

MAKES ABOUT 700 g (1½ lb)

Oil an 18 cm (7 inch) square tin. Put the sugar, milk and butter in a large heavy saucepan and heat gently until the sugar has dissolved, stirring continuously. The large grains of sugar are slow to dissolve, so take this stage carefully. Bring to the boil and boil to 115°C (240°F), stirring occasionally.

Remove the pan from the heat, stir in the vanilla essence and beat well until thick and creamy.

Pour the mixture into the prepared tin. Leave to cool. Mark into squares as it begins to set. When completely cold and set, turn the fudge out and cut into the marked squares.

Peanut Penuche

Salted peanuts and peanut butter are used to obtain the delicious rich flavour of this fudge. The nuts are roughly chopped only to provide a good contrast in texture.

450 g (1 lb) light soft brown sugar
175 ml (6 fl oz) milk
50 g (2 oz) smooth peanut butter

50 g (2 oz) salted peanuts, roughly chopped

MAKES ABOUT 700 g (1½ lb)

Lightly oil an 18 cm (7 inch) square tin. Put the sugar, milk and peanut butter in a large, heavy saucepan and heat gently until the sugar has dissolved, stirring continuously. Bring to the boil and boil to 115°C (240°F), stirring occasionally.

Remove the pan from the heat, stir in the chopped peanuts and beat well until thickened.

Pour the mixture into the prepared tin. Leave to cool. Mark into squares as it begins to set. When completely cold and set, turn the fudge out and cut into the marked squares.

Rum and Raisin Fudge

Rum-soaked raisins are always a popular flavouring. In this fudge recipe, the raisins are left to steep in the rum for 2 hours.

60 ml (4 tbsp) seedless raisins
30 ml (2 tbsp) rum
450 g (1 lb) granulated sugar
225 g (8 oz) soft dark brown sugar

250 ml (9 fl oz) single cream
30 ml (2 tbsp) golden syrup

MAKES ABOUT 900 g (2 lb)

Put the raisins and rum in a small bowl and leave to soak for about 2 hours. Just before making the fudge, oil an 18 cm (7 inch) square tin.

Put the sugars, cream and golden syrup in a large, heavy saucepan and heat gently until the sugars have dissolved, stirring continuously. Bring to the boil and boil to 115°C (240°F), stirring occasionally.

Remove the pan from the heat and stir in the rum and raisins. Cool a little, then beat until the mixture starts to leave a trail on itself.

Pour the fudge into the prepared tin. Leave to cool. Mark into squares as it begins to set. When completely cold and set, turn the fudge out and cut into the marked squares.

top SOUR CREAM AND BRANDIED APRICOT FUDGE (page 64); bottom CREAM AND CHERRY FUDGE (page 65)

Chocolate and Peppermint Fudge

This fudge has a lovely, soft texture. Its superb flavour is obtained by the addition of plain dessert chocolate and oil of peppermint. Avoid using peppermint flavouring as this is a synthetic substitute and the taste of the fudge will be impaired.

450 g (1 lb) granulated sugar	100 g (4 oz) plain chocolate, grated
150 ml (¼ pint) milk	2 drops oil of peppermint
60 ml (4 tbsp) clear honey	
150 g (5 oz) butter	MAKES ABOUT 700 g (1½ lb)

Lightly oil an 18 cm (7 inch) square tin. Put the sugar, milk, honey and butter in a large, heavy saucepan and heat gently until the sugar has dissolved, stirring continuously. Bring to the boil and boil to 115°C (240°F), stirring occasionally.

Remove the pan from the heat and leave on a cold surface, without stirring, for 5 minutes. Add the chocolate and oil of peppermint and beat in until the chocolate is melted and the mixture starts to leave a trail on itself.

Pour the fudge into the prepared tin. Leave to cool. Mark into squares as it begins to set. When completely cold and set, turn the fudge out and cut into the marked squares.

Fruit and Nut Cream Fudge

The fruit and nuts in this tempting fudge recipe are raisins and toasted hazelnuts. After browning, the nuts are chopped, and provide a good texture contrast to the creamy fudge.

40 g (1½ oz) shelled hazelnuts	250 ml (9 fl oz) single cream
45 ml (3 tbsp) seedless raisins	few drops of vanilla essence
700 g (1½ lb) granulated sugar	
30 ml (2 tbsp) golden syrup	MAKES ABOUT 900 g (2 lb)

Spread the nuts on a baking sheet and lightly toast under the grill or in the oven at 200°C (400°F) mark 6 for 5–10 minutes. Rub the nuts in a clean teatowel to remove the skins. Chop them and mix with the raisins in a small bowl. Lightly oil an 18 cm (7 inch) square tin.

Put the sugar, golden syrup and cream in a large, heavy saucepan and heat gently until the sugar has dissolved, stirring continuously. Bring to the boil and boil to 115°C (240°F), stirring occasionally.

Remove the pan from the heat, wait for the bubbles to subside and beat in the nuts and raisins and vanilla essence. Cool a little, then beat until the mixture starts to leave a trail on itself.

Pour the fudge into the prepared tin. Leave to cool. Mark into squares as it begins to set. When completely cold and set, turn the fudge out and cut into the marked squares.

Honey and Chocolate Fudge

The honey used in this recipe not only gives the fudge flavour, but stops it crystallising as well – making it deliciously soft and creamy textured.

450 g (1 lb) granulated sugar
45 ml (3 tbsp) clear honey
450 ml (¾ pint) sweetened condensed milk
100 g (4 oz) butter

100 g (4 oz) plain chocolate, grated
few drops of vanilla essence

MAKES ABOUT 700 g (1½ lb)

Oil a 20 cm (8 inch) square tin. Put the sugar, honey, condensed milk and butter in a large, heavy saucepan and heat gently until the butter has melted and the sugar completely dissolved, stirring continuously. Bring to the boil and boil to 115°C (240°F), stirring occasionally.

Remove the pan from the heat and beat in the chocolate and vanilla essence. Cool a little, then beat until the mixture starts to leave a trail on itself.

Pour the fudge into the prepared tin. Leave to cool. Mark into squares as it begins to set. When completely cold and set, turn the fudge out and cut into the marked squares.

Drambuie Dream

Drambuie, a whisky and honey liqueur, turns this creamy fudge into an alcoholic dream – the perfect Christmas present.

700 g (1½ lb) granulated sugar
300 ml (½ pint) single cream

30 ml (2 tbsp) clear honey
15 ml (1 tbsp) Drambuie

MAKES ABOUT 900 g (2 lb)

Oil an 18 cm (7 inch) square tin. Put the sugar, cream and honey in a large, heavy saucepan and heat gently until the sugar has dissolved, stirring continuously. Bring to the boil and boil to 115°C (240°F), stirring occasionally, paying particular attention to the base of the pan in case the creamy mixture burns.

Remove the pan from the heat, wait for the bubbles to subside and stir in the Drambuie. Cool a little, then beat until the mixture starts to leave a trail on itself.

Pour the fudge into the prepared tin. Leave to cool. Mark into squares as it begins to set. When completely cold and set, turn the fudge out and cut into the marked squares.

Cashew Nut Fudge

Cashews have a light, subtle flavour often neglected by sweet makers; toasting helps to emphasise it a little.

50 g (2 oz) shelled cashew
  nuts
450 g (1 lb) granulated
  sugar
150 ml (¼ pint)
  sweetened condensed
  milk

150 ml (¼ pint) fresh milk
100 g (4 oz) butter
few drops of vanilla
  essence

MAKES ABOUT 700 g (1½ lb)

Oil an 18 cm (7 inch) square tin. Spread the cashews on a baking sheet. Lightly toast them under the grill or in the oven at 200°C (400°F) mark 6 for 5–10 minutes. Leave to cool, then split the nuts lengthways along the natural break.

Put the sugar, milks and butter in a large, heavy saucepan and heat gently until the sugar has dissolved, stirring continuously. Bring to the boil and boil to 115°C (240°F), stirring occasionally.

Remove the pan from the heat, add the toasted nuts and vanilla essence, then beat just until the mixture leaves a trail on itself.

Pour the fudge into the prepared tin. Leave to cool. Mark into squares as it begins to set. When completely cold and set, turn the fudge out and cut into the marked squares.

top ALMOND TOFFEE (page 69);
bottom TREACLE TOFFEE (page 69)

Sour Cream Honey Fudge

You need an especially large saucepan for making this fudge as the mixture froths up as it cooks: do not use a pan less than 4 litre (7 pint) capacity.

350 ml (12 fl oz) soured cream	45 ml (3 tbsp) clear honey
4 ml (¾ tsp) bicarbonate of soda	40 g (1½ oz) butter, cut into small pieces
700 g (1½ lb) granulated sugar	MAKES ABOUT 900 g (2 lb)

Lightly oil an 18 cm (7 inch) square tin. Put the soured cream, bicarbonate of soda, sugar and honey in a large, heavy saucepan. Stir well and leave to stand for about 20 minutes. Heat gently until the sugar has dissolved, stirring continuously. Bring to the boil and boil to 114°C (238°F), stirring occasionally.

Remove the pan from the heat, stir in the pieces of butter and leave to stand for 5 minutes. Then beat until the mixture starts to leave a trail on itself.

Pour the fudge into the prepared tin. Leave to cool. Mark into squares as it begins to set. When completely cold and set, turn the fudge out and cut into the marked squares.

Sour Cream and Brandied Apricot Fudge

Soak 50 g (2 oz) roughly chopped dried apricots in 60 ml (4 tbsp) brandy overnight. Make as for Sour Cream Honey Fudge, beating in the apricots and brandy at the end. The large quantity of brandy makes this into rather a sticky, rich fudge.

Devon Cream Fudge

Anyone who has ever spent a holiday in the West Country will recognise the special flavour of clotted cream in this rich fudge.

700 g (1½ lb) granulated sugar	few drops of vanilla essence
175 ml (6 fl oz) clotted cream	MAKES ABOUT 900 g (2 lb)
300 ml (½ pint) fresh milk	

Oil an 18 cm (7 inch) square tin. Put the sugar, cream and milk into a large, heavy saucepan and heat gently until the sugar has completely dissolved, stirring continuously. Bring to the boil and boil to 115°C (240°F), stirring occasionally to prevent the milk and cream burning on the base of the pan. As the mixture nears the correct temperature, lower the heat a little.

As soon as the temperature reaches 115°C (240°F), remove the pan from the heat and stir in the vanilla essence. Wait until the bubbles subside, then beat until the mixture starts to leave a trail on itself.

Pour the fudge into the prepared tin. Leave to cool. Mark into squares as it begins to set. When completely cold and set, turn the fudge out and cut into the marked squares.

Devon Cream and Cherry Fudge

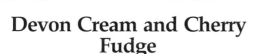

Make as for Devon Cream Fudge and add 75 ml (5 tbsp) chopped maraschino cherries when you beat it. (Dry the cherries well on absorbent kitchen paper before you chop them.) This mixture is rather slow to set. Leave overnight before turning the fudge out.

MAKES ABOUT 900 g (2 lb)

Pineapple Cream Fudge

This fudge has an unusual combination of flavour and texture. Pineapple essence and glacé pineapple are both used: you could, if you wish, make your own glacé fruit (see page 94).

700 g (1½ lb) granulated sugar	few drops of pineapple essence
75 g (3 oz) butter	60 ml (4 tbsp) chopped glacé pineapple
200 ml (7 fl oz) evaporated milk	
200 ml (7 fl oz) fresh milk	MAKES ABOUT 900 g (2 lb)

Oil an 18 cm (7 inch) square tin. Put the sugar, butter and milks in a large, heavy saucepan and heat gently until the sugar has dissolved, stirring continuously. Bring to the boil and boil to 115°C (240°F), stirring occasionally.

Remove the pan from the heat and stir in the pineapple essence and chopped pineapple. Cool a little, then beat until the mixture starts to leave a trail on itself.

Pour the fudge into the prepared tin. Leave to cool. Mark into squares as it begins to cool. When completely cold and set, turn the fudge out and cut into the marked squares.

Date Squares

The higher-than-normal temperature used in this recipe gives a crisper textured fudge.

450 g (1 lb) granulated sugar	few drops of vanilla essence
150 ml (¼ pint) milk	60 ml (4 tbsp) chopped dates
150 ml (¼ pint) sweetened condensed milk	
100 g (4 oz) butter	MAKES ABOUT 700 g (1½ lb)

Oil an 18 cm (7 inch) square tin. Put the sugar, milks and butter in a large, heavy saucepan and heat gently until the sugar has dissolved, stirring continuously. Bring to the boil and boil, still stirring, to 121°C (250°F). Start boiling fairly quickly then lower the temperature and boil it very slowly towards the end.

Remove the pan from the heat, add the vanilla and dates and beat until the mixture starts to thicken and grain.

Pour the fudge into the prepared tin. Leave to cool. Mark into squares as it begins to set. When completely cold and set, turn the fudge out and cut into the marked squares.

Canada Cream Fudge

This tempting fudge, made with maple syrup, has a crisp texture. Make sure you use real maple syrup, not maple-flavoured syrup.

450 ml (¾ pint) maple syrup
15 ml (1 tbsp) golden syrup
150 ml (¼ pint) single cream

5 ml (1 tsp) vanilla essence

MAKES ABOUT 450 g (1 lb)

Oil a 15 cm (6 inch) round tin. Put the syrups and cream in a large, heavy saucepan and bring very slowly to the boil, stirring continuously. Boil to 114°C (238°F), without stirring.

Remove the pan from the heat, cool for 2 minutes then add the vanilla essence. Beat until the mixture starts to thicken.

Pour the fudge into the prepared tin. Leave to cool. Mark into diamonds as it begins to set. When completely cold and set, turn the fudge out and cut into the marked shapes.

Mocha Fudge

Chocolate and coffee are a traditional mixture in confectionery. If you prefer to use pure coffee essence you should reduce the quantity to about 5 ml (1 tsp), but the texture of the fudge will be much drier.

700 g (1½ lb) granulated sugar
45 ml (3 tbsp) golden syrup
175 ml (6 fl oz) milk
75 g (3 oz) plain chocolate, broken into small pieces

pinch of salt
30 ml (2 tbsp) chicory and coffee essence
75 g (3 oz) butter, cut into small pieces

MAKES ABOUT 900 g (2 lb)

Oil an 18 cm (7 inch) square tin. Put all the ingredients except the butter in a large, heavy saucepan and heat gently until the sugar has dissolved, stirring continuously. Bring to the boil and boil to 113°C (236°F), stirring occasionally.

Remove the pan from the heat, add the pieces of butter and leave to stand for 5 minutes. Beat until the mixture starts to leave a trail on itself.

Pour the fudge into the prepared tin. Leave to cool. Mark into squares as it begins to set. When completely cold and set, turn out and cut into the marked squares.

BUTTERSCOTCH (page 72)

Toffees and Boiled Sweets

OFFEES are family-style sweets – hardly elegant but none the less delicious. Real old fashioned toffees are not common now, but they are very popular on the odd occasion when they do appear. Made by boiling the sugar to very high temperatures, in the 143–154°C (290–310°F) region, they are brittle and the simple versions are clear and shiny. True toffees are so hard that you cannot cut them into neat pieces. They have to be broken with a hammer, so that the pieces all come out different shapes and sizes. When sucked they are inclined to go extremely chewy! For a gift, do not try and wrap individual pieces of old fashioned toffee. Pack them in a square box in layers, between sheets of waxed paper or baking parchment. They make a fun gift on Hallowe'en or Bonfire Night.

Caramels are softer, often with cream or butter added for flavour. The temperature used to make them is not usually quite so high as that for toffee, so they are less brittle and can be cut up neatly. They are less hard on the teeth than true toffees, and are my personal favourites in this chapter. Then there is a whole range of boiled sweets, all immensely popular and fun to make – barley sugar, mints and humbugs plus a wide variety of other possible flavours.

The temperature and humidity in the kitchen are important for all confectionery, but more so for toffees and boiled sweets. In a damp atmosphere, toffees go sticky and cling to each other disastrously. So choose a dry day and try to keep the kitchen temperature at a comfortable 15–18°C (60–65°F).

If possible, use an aluminium pan for making toffees and boiled sweets. The temperatures are so high that it is all too easy to burn the syrup – aluminium will give the most even heat distribution and the best possible chance of avoiding scorching. As always, heat the sugar gently until dissolved, then raise the heat and keep it as even as possible until the required temperature is reached. Once the sugar has dissolved, do not stir unless the recipe specifically says to do so – stirring encourages the sugar to grain and the sweets will be cloudy.

'Pulling', on the other hand, is a technique specially designed to make the sweets opaque. If you tip the hot syrup on to a baking sheet instead of into a small tin, and allow it to cool a little, it can then be folded and pulled, twisted and generally handled until it becomes silky and quite different to look at. But do use rubber gloves for this process, as the mixture may still be very hot in the middle even if it seems to be cooling outside.

When you are pulling and twisting toffees, work quickly. One minute the mixture will be all soft and floppy, the next it will have hardened

too much to cut. If possible have someone else standing by to help so that one of you can pull and twist while the other cuts. If the mixture does set before you have cut it, the toffee is not wasted. Put it on the baking sheet in a low oven for 3–4 minutes and you can work it again.

Store toffees and boiled sweets in a dry atmosphere at an even temperature. Cellophane wrappers and glass jars are often the most attractive way to present them.

Almond Toffee

A hard, golden toffee, packed with nuts. Ready-blanched almonds can be used but the flavour will not be as good.

150 g (5 oz) shelled almonds	few drops of almond essence
450 g (1 lb) granulated sugar	MAKES ABOUT 550 g (1¼ lb)
300 ml (½ pint) water	
pinch of cream of tartar	

Blanch the almonds in a bowl of boiling water for about 10 minutes. Cut them crossways into halves. Dry thoroughly in a low oven, but without allowing them to brown.

Oil an 18 cm (7 inch) square tin. Put the sugar and water in a large, heavy saucepan and heat gently until the sugar has dissolved, stirring continuously. Dissolve the cream of tartar in 10 ml (2 tsp) cold water and stir into the syrup. Bring to the boil and boil to 137°C (280°F).

Remove the pan from the heat and stir in the halved almonds and a few drops of almond essence. Quickly pour the toffee into the prepared tin. Cool.

When completely hardened, turn the toffee out and break into pieces, using a small hammer or a rolling pin.

Treacle Toffee

This is a traditional hard, black toffee with a strong molasses flavour. It should be broken into pieces, using a small hammer. Old fashioned kitchens were equipped with a toffee hammer for this purpose – about the size you might use for model making.

450 g (1 lb) soft dark brown sugar	150 ml (¼ pint) sweetened condensed milk
100 g (4 oz) black treacle	15 ml (1 tbsp) vinegar
100 g (4 oz) golden syrup	
50 g (2 oz) unsalted butter	MAKES ABOUT 700 g (1½ lb)

Oil a 28×18 cm (11×7 inch) baking tin. Put all the ingredients in a large, heavy saucepan and heat gently until the sugar has dissolved, stirring continuously. Bring to the boil and boil, without stirring, to 137°C (280°F). Pour into the prepared tin. Leave to cool.

When completely hardened, turn the toffee out on to a board and break roughly into pieces, using a small hammer.

Rum Honeycomb Toffee

A lovely dark colour underneath, this toffee is clear as a jewel, with delightful, golden honeycombing on top.

450 g (1 lb) granulated sugar	2.5 ml (½ tsp) bicarbonate of soda
45 ml (3 tbsp) golden syrup	5 ml (1 tsp) rum essence
15 ml (1 tbsp) vinegar	MAKES ABOUT 350 g (12 oz)
150 ml (¼ pint) water	

Oil an 18 cm (7 inch) square tin. Put the sugar, golden syrup, vinegar and water in a large, heavy saucepan and heat gently until the sugar has dissolved, stirring continuously. Bring to the boil, without stirring, and boil to 154°C (310°F).

When the mixture reaches 153°C (308°F), remove from the heat, dissolve the bicarbonate of soda in the rum essence and 10 ml (2 tsp) water and stir in. Make sure the temperature has risen to 154°C (310°F) and quickly pour the toffee into the prepared tin.

When completely hardened, turn the toffee out and break into pieces with a hammer. Store in layers between sheets of waxed paper or parchment in an airtight container.

Honeycomb Toffee

A lovely crystal-clear amber toffee with a layer of yellow honeycombing on top.

450 g (1 lb) granulated sugar	2.5 ml (½ tsp) bicarbonate of soda
300 ml (½ pint) water	
60 ml (4 tbsp) malt vinegar	MAKES ABOUT 450 g (1 lb)

Oil an 18 cm (7 inch) square tin. Put the sugar, water and vinegar in a large, heavy saucepan and heat gently until the sugar has dissolved, stirring continuously. Bring to the boil and boil, without stirring, to 140°C (285°F).

Remove the pan from the heat. Dissolve the bicarbonate of soda in 10 ml (2 tsp) water and stir into the toffee. Quickly pour the syrup into the prepared tin.

When the toffee is sufficiently set, mark it into small squares with a knife. When hardened, turn the toffee out and break along the marks.

Peppermint Toffee

Old-fashioned toffees have rather gone out of style these days, which is a pity because they are really very good.

450 g (1 lb) granulated sugar	15 ml (1 tbsp) vinegar
150 ml (¼ pint) water	few drops of oil of peppermint
100 g (4 oz) unsalted butter	MAKES ABOUT 450 g (1 lb)

Oil an 18 cm (7 inch) square tin. Put the sugar, water, butter and vinegar in a large, heavy saucepan and heat gently until the sugar has dissolved, stirring continuously. Bring to the boil and boil, without stirring, to 126°C (260°F). Add a little oil of peppermint and continue boiling to 137°C (280°F).

Remove the pan from the heat and quickly pour the toffee into the prepared tin. Mark into squares with a knife as it begins to harden.

When completely hardened, turn the toffee out and break along the marks. Wrap in twists of waxed paper or parchment and store in an airtight container.

Pulled Toffee

The process of turning a clear syrup into this silky toffee, simply by folding and manipulating it, is absolutely fascinating. Children will love to watch you, but do keep them at a safe distance from the hot mixture.

450 g (1 lb) granulated sugar	pinch of cream of tartar
150 ml (¼ pint) water	MAKES ABOUT 550 g (1¼ lb)
100 g (4 oz) butter	

Oil a baking sheet. Put the sugar, water, butter and cream of tartar into a large, heavy saucepan and heat gently until the sugar has dissolved, stirring continuously. Bring to the boil and boil, without stirring, to 137°C (280°F). Quickly pour the mixture on to the prepared sheet and leave until you can handle it with rubber gloves.

Oil the rubber gloves, then fold the sides of the toffee to the middle and pull it out again. Keep folding and pulling until the toffee turns silky looking and opaque. Twist into long strips and cut into pieces with scissors. Leave to cool.

When completely cold and hard, wrap in twists of waxed paper, parchment, cellophane or coloured foil.

Pulled Peppermint Toffee

Add a few drops of oil of peppermint to the Pulled Toffee recipe, just before pouring it on to the baking sheet.

Aniseed Toffee

Add 1.25 ml (¼ tsp) oil of aniseed to the Pulled Toffee recipe, just before pouring on to the baking sheet. This gives only a light flavour of aniseed. You could add more if you like a really strong taste.

Butterscotch

Butterscotch is a time-honoured favourite, and this recipe has a particularly good buttery taste.

65 g (2½ oz) butter, cut into small pieces	60 ml (4 tbsp) golden syrup
450 g (1 lb) soft light brown sugar	300 ml (½ pint) water

MAKES ABOUT 450 g (1 lb)

Oil an 18 cm (7 inch) square tin. Put the butter, sugar, syrup and water into a large, heavy saucepan and heat gently until the sugar has dissolved, stirring continuously. Bring to the boil, without stirring, and boil to 143°C (290°F), stirring just once or twice to make sure the butter is not sticking and burning on the bottom of the pan.

Remove the pan from the heat, stir lightly and pour into the prepared tin. Leave to cool. Mark into squares with a sharp knife as it begins to set. When completely cold and set, turn the butterscotch out of the tin and break along the marked lines.

Cream Caramels

The creamy flavour of these popular caramels is unmistakeable, and they are deliciously chewy too.

450 g (1 lb) granulated sugar	150 ml (¼ pint) single cream
100 g (4 oz) powdered glucose	25 g (1 oz) unsalted butter
215 ml (7½ fl oz) water	MAKES ABOUT 550 g (1¼ lb)

Oil an 18 cm (7 inch) square tin. Put the sugar, glucose and water in a large, heavy saucepan and heat gently until the sugar has dissolved, stirring continuously. Bring to the boil, without stirring, and boil to 129°C (265°F).

Meanwhile, put the cream and butter in a small pan and heat gently to melt the butter. Add the cream and butter mixture to the syrup and boil again, stirring this time, until the temperature returns to 129°C (265°F).

Remove the pan from the heat and pour the mixture into the prepared tin. Mark the caramel into squares as it begins to set.

When completely cold and set, turn the caramel out and break along the marked lines. Wrap each piece in waxed paper or parchment. Leave to mature for two to three days before eating.

Vanilla Cream Caramels

When matured, these caramels are softer than the previous Cream Caramel recipe, chewy but not so hard on your teeth.

350 g (12 oz) granulated sugar
20 ml (2 tbsp) powdered glucose
225 g (8 oz) butter
150 ml (¼ pint) milk

150 ml (¼ pint) single cream
10 ml (2 tsp) vanilla essence

MAKES 550 g (1¼ lb)

Lightly oil a 20 cm (8 inch) square tin. Put the sugar, glucose, one third of the butter and all the milk in a large, heavy saucepan. Heat gently until the sugar has dissolved, stirring continuously. Still stirring, bring to the boil and add half the remaining butter. Boil, stirring, to 112°C (235°F). Meanwhile, warm the cream slightly in a separate pan. Cut the remaining butter into small pieces.

Remove the pan from the heat and stir in the warmed cream, vanilla essence and remaining pieces of butter. Boil the mixture to 121°C (250°F).

Pour the mixture into the prepared tin. Leave to cool. Mark into small squares as it begins to set.

When completely set, turn the caramel out and break into squares along the marked lines. Wrap each square in waxed paper or parchment. Leave to mature for several days before eating.

Chocolate Coated Caramels

These milk chocolate-coated caramels are very soft and sticky when first made, and should be left for about two days to mature before eating.

450 g (1 lb) granulated sugar
150 ml (¼ pint) water
100 g (4 oz) powdered glucose
150 ml (¼ pint) single cream

25 g (1 oz) unsalted butter
450 g (1 lb) milk chocolate

MAKES ABOUT 900 g (2 lb)

Oil an 18 cm (7 inch) square tin. Put the sugar and water in a large, heavy saucepan and heat gently until the sugar has dissolved, stirring continuously. Stir in the glucose, bring to the boil and boil, without stirring, to 115°C (240°F).

Meanwhile, put the cream and butter in a small pan and heat gently to melt the butter.

When the syrup reaches 115°C (240°F), lower the heat slightly and add the warmed cream and butter mixture. Stir gently and continue boiling to 121°C (250°F).

Pour the mixture into the prepared tin. Leave to cool. As soon as the caramel is firm enough to handle, turn it out of the tin and cut into very small squares with scissors. Once out of the tin the caramel will spread a little, and the pieces will end up bigger than you first cut them.

Break the chocolate into a bowl and melt it over a pan of hot water. Using a dipping ring, dip the caramels one at a time in the chocolate to give a generous coating. Place on parchment to harden. Leave to mature for two to three days before eating.

Chocolate Caramels

It makes a delicious change to flavour the caramels with chocolate instead of coating them in chocolate.

40 g (1½ oz) unsalted butter
150 ml (¼ pint) sweetened condensed milk
225 g (8 oz) granulated sugar
150 ml (¼ pint) golden syrup
15 ml (1 tbsp) powdered glucose
50 g (2 oz) plain chocolate, grated
few drops of vanilla essence

MAKES ABOUT 450 g (1 lb)

Oil an 18 cm (7 inch) square tin. Put the butter in a large, heavy pan and melt it slowly. Add the condensed milk, sugar, golden syrup and glucose and heat gently until the sugar has dissolved, stirring continuously. Bring to the boil and boil to 110°C (230°F), stirring occasionally. Stir in the grated chocolate and boil to 123°C (255°F), stirring.

Remove the pan from the heat and stir in a few drops of vanilla essence. Pour the mixture into the prepared tin. Leave to cool. Mark into squares with a knife as it begins to set.

When completely cold and set, turn the caramel out and break into squares along the marked lines. Wrap each square in waxed paper or parchment. Leave for two to three days to mature before eating.

Old Fashioned Humbugs

You can be quite generous with the colouring for this recipe as a strong colour contrast makes the sweets look especially good.

450 g (1 lb) granulated sugar
100 g (4 oz) powdered glucose
2.5 ml (½ tsp) cream of tartar
300 ml (½ pint) water
1.25 ml (¼ tsp) oil of peppermint
brown food colouring

MAKES ABOUT 450 g (1 lb)

Lightly oil two baking sheets. Put the sugar, glucose, cream of tartar and water in a large, heavy saucepan and heat gently until the sugar has dissolved, stirring continuously. Bring to the boil, without stirring, and boil to 143°C (290°F).

Remove the pan from the heat and add the oil of peppermint. Pour half the syrup on to each prepared baking sheet. Add about 2.5 ml (½ tsp) brown colouring to one portion. Leave until cool enough to handle.

Wearing oiled rubber gloves, fold and pull each portion until they become opaque and are starting to set. Roll each one into a long rod.

Lay the portions side by side and twist them together. Using scissors, cut off in 1 cm (½ inch) lengths. If the sugar sets hard before you have finished shaping it, put the baking sheet in the oven at 130°C (250°F) mark ½ for 3–4 minutes until the mixture becomes workable again. When completely cold, wrap each piece in cellophane.

CHOCOLATE BRANDY TRUFFLES (page 80)

Fruit Drops

The icing sugar in this recipe stops the fruit drops sticking together, so pack them straight into a glass jar for maximum effect.

450 g (1 lb) granulated
  sugar
100 g (4 oz) powdered
  glucose
5 ml (1 tsp) cream of
  tartar
175 ml (6 fl oz) water
2.5 ml (½ tsp) oil of
  lemon

yellow food colouring
2.5 ml (½ tsp) oil of
  orange
orange food colouring
icing sugar

MAKES ABOUT 450 g (1 lb)

Lightly oil two baking sheets. Put the sugar, glucose, cream of tartar and water in a large, heavy saucepan and heat gently until the sugar has dissolved, stirring continuously. Bring to the boil and boil, without stirring, to 154°C (310°F).

Remove the pan from the heat and divide the syrup between the prepared baking sheets. Add about 2.5 ml (½ tsp) oil of lemon and a few drops of yellow food colouring to one portion, and about 2.5 ml (½ tsp) oil of orange and a few drops of orange colouring to the other. Leave until cool enough to handle.

Sift some icing sugar into a bowl. Wearing oiled rubber gloves, fold and pull one portion to mix in the flavouring and colouring, then roll it into a stick. Cut off small portions with scissors and roll them between your hands to make small balls. Drop the balls in the icing sugar to coat lightly, then remove them to cool.

Repeat with the other portion. If by the time you have worked the first batch the other has hardened too much to handle, put the baking sheet in the oven at 130°C (250°F) mark ½ for 3–4 minutes until the mixture becomes workable again.

Clear Mints

These cool, clear mints have a lovely light green colour. Remember to handle the mixture quickly as soon as it begins to set, before it gets too hard to cut.

450 g (1 lb) granulated
  sugar
175 ml (6 fl oz) water
100 g (4 oz) powdered
  glucose

2.5 ml (½ tsp) peppermint
  essence
few drops of green food
  colouring

MAKES ABOUT 550 g (1¼ lb)

Lightly oil a shallow tin measuring about 28×18 cm (11×7 inches). Put the sugar and water in a heavy saucepan and heat gently until the sugar has dissolved, stirring continuously. Stir in the glucose, bring to the boil and boil, without stirring, to 154°C (310°F).

Remove the pan from the heat and stir in the peppermint essence and a few drops of green food colouring.

Pour the syrup into the prepared tin. Leave to cool. As soon as the mint is firm enough to handle, turn it out with the help of a palette knife and cut into squares with scissors.

Barley Sugar Twists

Many modern barley sugars are flavoured only with lemon. This traditional recipe is made with real barley water.

30 ml (2 tbsp) pearl barley
1.2 litres (2 pints) water
pared rind and juice of
 ½ lemon
450 g (1 lb) granulated
 sugar

pinch of cream of tartar

MAKES ABOUT 450 g (1 lb)

Put the pearl barley in a saucepan with 300 ml (½ pint) of the cold water and bring to the boil. Drain and rinse under cold running water. Put the barley back in the pan with 900 ml (1½ pints) cold water and the lemon rind. Bring to the boil again, cover and simmer for about 2 hours.

Strain the barley liquid into a measuring jug, add the lemon juice and make the liquid up to 600 ml (1 pint) with cold water. Lightly oil a baking sheet.

Put the sugar, cream of tartar and barley water in a large, heavy saucepan and heat gently until the sugar has dissolved, stirring continuously. Bring to the boil and boil to 143°C (290°F).

Remove the pan from the heat and quickly pour the syrup on to the prepared baking sheet. Tilt the sheet to spread it evenly. Leave to cool a little.

As soon as the barley sugar is firm enough to handle, cut it into strips with scissors and twist each strip. Place on a board to finish cooling. The outside cools quicker than the middle, so work from both sides towards the middle, not straight from one side to the other. Wrap in twists of clear cellophane and store in a glass jar with an airtight stopper.

Buttered Brazils

Sweet, moist, fresh nuts are best for these sweets.

225 g (8 oz) demerara
 sugar
50 g (2 oz) butter
10 ml (2 tsp) powdered
 glucose

pinch of cream of tartar
90 ml (6 tbsp) water
50 g (2 oz) shelled Brazil
 nuts

MAKES ABOUT 350 g (12 oz)

Lightly oil a baking sheet. Put the sugar, butter, glucose, cream of tartar and water in a small, heavy saucepan and heat gently until the sugar has dissolved, stirring continuously. Bring to the boil and boil to 137°C (280°F), stirring occasionally.

Remove the pan from the heat. Using a dipping ring, quickly dip each nut into the mixture and place on the prepared baking sheet. Work as quickly as you can and reheat the syrup if necessary to keep it liquid. Leave until cold, then remove the buttered Brazils from the baking sheet and place in paper sweet cases.

Petits Fours

HOWEVER good the dinner, a few petits fours offered with the coffee will make guests feel just that little bit pampered. But they are a fiddle to make, on top of everything else, so any hostess will delight in a gift box, all ready to pass round. Pack a selection of fancy and plain ones together for best effect.

Marzipan Fruits

This is an excellent smooth paste, easy to mould and shape into fruits. The uncooked almond paste in the Almond-filled Fruits recipe is easier to make, but not so easy to mould, and it quickly cracks as it dries out.

450 g (1 lb) granulated sugar	2 egg whites
150 ml (¼ pint) water	75 g (3 oz) icing sugar
pinch of cream of tartar	a range of food colourings
350 g (12 oz) ground almonds	

Lightly oil a baking sheet. Put the sugar and water in a large, heavy saucepan and heat gently until the sugar has dissolved, stirring continuously. Bring to the boil, without stirring. Dissolve the cream of tartar in a little cold water, stir it into the syrup and continue boiling to 115°C (240°F).

Remove the pan from the heat and beat until the sugar starts to grain. Stir in the ground almonds and egg whites. Cook gently over a low heat for a few minutes, stirring well.

Pour the mixture on to the prepared baking sheet. Sift over the icing sugar and mix in, using a wooden spatula. When cool enough to handle, knead by hand until the paste is soft and pliable, adding a little extra icing sugar if necessary.

When the marzipan is cold and smooth, break off small pieces and mould into tiny apples, bananas, oranges and so on. Use fine paint brushes and edible food colourings to tint them.

If you wish, you can knead colouring into a larger amount of marzipan to make the basis of several fruits. For example, colour the marzipan yellow for bananas, green for apples, orange for oranges. After shaping, add shading to make each individual fruit more attractive. Leave to dry, then place in paper petits four cases. Store in an airtight container.

Almond-filled Fruits

Quick and easy to make and unfailingly popular. Use dried or candied stone fruits, which have a good cavity when the stone is removed.

100 g (4 oz) icing sugar	1 egg, lightly beaten
100 g (4 oz) caster sugar	a selection of dried or candied fruits, eg. dates, figs, candied apricots etc
225 g (8 oz) ground almonds	
2.5 ml (½ tsp) rum essence	caster sugar

Sift the icing sugar into a bowl and mix in the caster sugar and almonds. Add the rum essence and enough of the egg to make a stiff paste. Knead by hand until smooth.

Press a small ball of almond paste into the centre of each fruit. Roll the filled fruits in caster sugar. Leave to dry a little. Place in paper petits four cases and store in an airtight container.

Chocolate Marzipan

Chocolate marzipan is made by kneading melted plain dessert chocolate into the almond paste. Wrap them in squares of coloured foil for maximum effect.

50 g (2 oz) icing sugar	few drops of ratafia
50 g (2 oz) caster sugar	essence
100 g (4 oz) ground	lemon juice
almonds	50 g (2 oz) plain chocolate
½ egg, size 3	
	MAKES FORTY

Sift the icing sugar into a bowl and mix in the caster sugar and almonds. Add the beaten egg, a few drops of ratafia essence and a little lemon juice and mix to a paste.

Break the chocolate into a bowl and melt it over a pan of hot water. Leave to cool, but not solidify, then add to the almond paste. Mix well, then knead by hand until smooth.

Roll out the marzipan to about 1 cm (½ inch) thick on a board dusted with drinking chocolate powder. Cut into squares, using a sharp knife.

Nutty Figs

If stored for long, the sugar coating soaks in and the figs no longer look so pretty, though they still taste good. For a gift, prepare them ahead and roll in sugar just before packing. If you use concentrated orange juice in the recipe, dilute it half and half with water.

450 g (1 lb) whole dried figs	100 g (4 oz) blanched almonds
300 ml (½ pint) orange juice	
strip of lemon rind	MAKES ABOUT 700 g (1½ lb)
100 g (4 oz) granulated sugar	

Put the figs in a saucepan with the orange juice, lemon rind and 25 g (1 oz) of the sugar. Heat gently until the sugar has dissolved. Bring to the boil and simmer for about 30–40 minutes until the figs are tender. Drain the figs and leave to cool.

Trim the stems off the figs and pierce the stem end of each one with a knife. Push an almond into the centre and close the opening again by pinching it together with your fingers.

Roll the figs in the remaining sugar. Put on a wire rack to dry thoroughly. Place in waxed paper cases and store in layers between waxed paper or parchment in an airtight container.

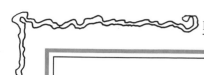

Marzipan Neapolitans

These are pretty to look at and much simpler to make than the fruit shapes. The texture is smooth and you can flavour the marzipan, if you like – rum essence is good.

225 g (8 oz) granulated sugar	1 egg white
65 ml (2½ fl oz) water	40 g (1½ oz) icing sugar
pinch of cream of tartar	pink and green food colourings
175 g (6 oz) ground almonds	
	MAKES ABOUT TWENTY SIX

Make the marzipan as for Marzipan Fruits (see page 78). Divide the marzipan into three portions. Tint one portion pale green, the second pink and leave the third portion plain.

Roll out each portion into a rectangle about 0.5 cm (¼ inch) thick measuring about 18×11 cm (7×4½ inches) on a board dusted with icing sugar. Brush off any excess icing sugar and carefully place them one on top of the other – putting the plain portion between the coloured ones. Using a sharp knife, trim the edges then cut the marzipan first into strips about 2.5 cm (1 inch) wide, then down into slices between 1 and 2 cm (½ and ¾ inch) thick. Place each one in a paper sweet case and store in an airtight container.

Chocolate Brandy Truffles

Rich and irresistible, these truffles are made with crushed praline, chocolate, coffee, brandy and cream, then rolled in chocolate vermicelli.

50 g (2 oz) unblanched almonds	100 g (4 oz) unsalted butter, cut into small pieces
50 g (2 oz) granulated sugar	45 ml (3 tbsp) double cream
350 g (12 oz) plain chocolate	chocolate vermicelli
100 ml (4 fl oz) strong black coffee	
15 ml (1 tbsp) brandy	MAKES ABOUT THIRTY

Lightly oil a baking sheet. Put the almonds and sugar in a small saucepan and heat very gently until the sugar has completely dissolved, stirring continuously. Increase the heat and boil until the sugar turns a rich golden caramel colour. Stir occasionally so the almonds colour evenly.

Tip the caramel on to the prepared baking sheet. Leave to cool. When cold, chop the praline roughly, then grind it to an even powder in a blender, food processor or nut mill.

Break the chocolate into a bowl, add the coffee and brandy and melt over a pan of hot water. Remove from the heat, cool a little then gradually add the butter. When well blended, leave to cool until the mixture will leave a trail on itself if lifted. Gently stir in the praline powder and cream. Put in the refrigerator for about 8 hours or overnight.

Take a teaspoon of the truffle mixture at a time and shape into balls. Roll them in chocolate vermicelli and leave to set. Store in a cool place.

Madeira Truffles

Freshly made, these truffles are quite spectacular. After two or three days storage they are still acceptable, but more ordinary. Madeira cake provides just the right crumb texture.

100 g (4 oz) ground almonds	about 45 ml (3 tbsp) Madeira
100 g (4 oz) cake crumbs	drinking chocolate powder
100 g (4 oz) caster sugar	
50 g (2 oz) apricot jam	MAKES ABOUT THIRTY

Put the ground almonds, cake crumbs and sugar in a bowl and mix together. Add enough apricot jam and Madeira to make a firmish mixture.

Take a small piece of the mixture at a time and roll into a ball. Toss the balls in drinking chocolate powder to coat them thoroughly. Place in paper petits four cases to harden. Store in an airtight container.

Langues de Chats à l'Orange

These tempting orange-flavoured, piped petits fours are fairly soft in texture, rather like Victoria sponge. They are best eaten on the day they are made.

50 g (2 oz) butter	50 g (2 oz) icing sugar, sifted
25 g (1 oz) caster sugar	75 g (3 oz) plain chocolate
½ egg	
grated rind and juice of ½ orange	MAKES ABOUT FIFTEEN
25 g (1 oz) plain flour	

Lightly oil a baking sheet. Cream 25 g (1 oz) of the butter and the caster sugar together in a bowl until pale and fluffy. Beat in the egg and half the orange rind. Work in the flour until the mixture is of a piping consistency.

Spoon the mixture into a piping bag fitted with a 1 cm (½ inch) plain nozzle. Pipe into fingers about 6 cm (2½ inches) long on the prepared baking sheet, keeping them well spaced apart as they will spread during cooking.

Bake in the oven at 220°C (425°F) mark 7 for about 5 minutes until the edges just start to colour. Lift on to a wire rack to cool.

Cream the rest of the butter and gradually beat in the icing sugar, remaining orange rind and enough juice to make a cream of spreading consistency. Sandwich the cold langues de chats in pairs with the butter cream, shaping the edges neatly.

Break the chocolate into a bowl and melt it over a pan of hot water. Dip both ends of each langue de chat generously in the chocolate. Leave to dry on greaseproof paper. Pack in an airtight container.

Hazelnut and Orange Meringues

These meringues are good served just as they are or they can be sandwiched with a little whipped cream. However, if you are giving them as a gift, remember that cream-filled meringues need eating within a few hours of assembling or they will go soft. If you are sure your gift will be eaten straight away, make them up 2–3 hours before presenting them, otherwise leave them plain.

40 g (1½ oz) shelled hazelnuts	100 g (4 oz) caster sugar
2 egg whites, size 3	few drops of oil of orange
pinch of salt	plain chocolate

MAKES TWENTY FOUR TO THIRTY

Brush two baking sheets lightly with oil and dust with sifted flour. Spread the hazelnuts on another baking sheet and lightly toast under a grill or in the oven at 200°C (400°F) mark 6 for about 10 minutes. Rub the nuts in a clean teatowel to remove the skins. Chop them finely and leave to cool. If you have used the oven to toast the nuts, reduce to the lowest possible temperature. If you used the grill, preheat the oven to about 70°C (150°F) mark low.

Put the egg whites in a bowl with the pinch of salt and whisk with an electric whisk until stiff but not dry. Whisk in a quarter of the sugar, 15 ml (1 tbsp) at a time. Change to a large balloon whisk and continue whisking by hand until the meringue is smooth and glossy. Add a few drops of oil of orange, the chopped nuts and remaining sugar and fold in evenly with a large metal spoon.

Using a teaspoon or a piping bag fitted with a piping nozzle about 0.5 cm (¼ inch) in diameter, shape tiny mounds of the meringue on the prepared baking sheets. Bake in the oven at the lowest possible temperature for 60–70 minutes until crisp on the outside but still slightly soft in the centre. Transfer the meringues to a wire rack to cool.

If desired the meringues may be coated in chocolate. Break the chocolate into a bowl and melt it over a pan of hot water. Add a few drops of oil of orange. Dip the top of each meringue in the chocolate, without covering it completely, and return to the wire rack to set. Store in an airtight container.

top ÉCLAIRS AU CAFÉ (page 86); bottom HAZELNUT AND ORANGE MERINGUES (above)

Almond and Coffee Meringues

Delicious, delicate little meringues, with a buttery covering topped with shiny icing.

1 egg white
25 g (1 oz) ground almonds
25 g (1 oz) caster sugar
15 g (½ oz) plain flour
15 g (½ oz) almonds, finely chopped, to decorate

Butter cream
75 g (3 oz) butter
175 g (6 oz) icing sugar
10 ml (2 tsp) instant coffee
15–30 ml (1–2 tbsp) hot water

Glacé icing
100 g (4 oz) icing sugar
10 ml (2 tsp) instant coffee
30 ml (2 tbsp) hot water

MAKES ABOUT EIGHTEEN

Lightly oil a baking sheet and dust with sifted flour. Whisk the egg white in a bowl until stiff and firm. Sift the ground almonds, caster sugar and flour together and fold into the egg white, using a metal spoon.

Spoon the mixture into a piping bag fitted with a 0.5 cm (¼ inch) plain round nozzle. Pipe the meringue mixture in 4 cm (1½ inch) lengths on to the prepared baking sheet. Bake in the oven at 190°C (375°F) mark 5 for 7–8 minutes. Lift on to a wire rack and leave to cool.

To make the butter cream, cream the butter until soft and gradually sift and beat in the icing sugar.

Dissolve the instant coffee in 15 ml (1 tbsp) of the hot water. Beat into the butter cream, add a little more hot water if necessary to achieve a working consistency.

Cover each meringue with a smooth mound of butter cream and leave to harden.

To make the icing, sift the icing sugar into a bowl. Dissolve the coffee in the hot water and gradually add to the icing sugar until the icing will coat the back of a spoon thickly.

Hold each meringue in your fingers and dip into the icing to coat the top and right down the sides, covering the butter cream. Put the iced meringues on a wire rack, decorate each one with a small pinch of chopped almonds and leave to set. Store in an airtight container.

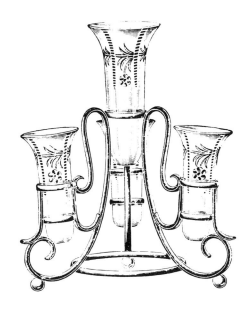

Almond and Pistachio Fingers

An intriguing blend of light, nutty flavours. Finely chopped pistachios are made into a paste with fragrant orange flower water, then sandwiched between a layer of almond paste and baked. Before cutting into fingers, the baked nut mixture is browned under the grill.

225 g (8 oz) ground almonds	100 g (4 oz) shelled pistachios
175 g (6 oz) icing sugar	15 ml (1 tbsp) orange flower water
15 ml (1 tbsp) rose water	
½ egg white	

MAKES TWENTY FOUR

Mix the ground almonds, icing sugar and rose water with a fork until they bind together. Add the egg white and continue to mix until a paste forms. Knead by hand until smooth.

Blanch the pistachios in a bowl of hot water for about 10 minutes. Remove the skins, then finely chop the nuts in a blender or food processor. Mix the pistachios and orange flower water to a paste.

Divide the almond paste in half. Spread half of it evenly over the base of an 18 cm (7 inch) square shallow tin, using your fingers to spread it to the corners. Spread the pistachio paste over the top. Cover with the remaining half of the almond paste, smoothing the surface with a palette knife.

Bake in the oven at 190°C (375°F) mark 5 for 10 minutes. Take the tin out of the oven and place under a hot grill for about 2 minutes to brown. Turn the almond and pistachio cake out into the grill pan and brown the other side. Leave to cool. When cold, cut into fingers. Store in an airtight container.

Palmiers

The secret of the shaping of these tempting pastries lies in the clever folding and cutting of the puff pastry.

100 g (4 oz) frozen puff pastry, thawed	icing sugar, for dusting
caster sugar, for dredging	MAKES EIGHTEEN

Roll out the pastry very thinly to a neat rectangle 15×20 cm (6×8 inches). Trim the edges straight with a sharp knife. Dredge the surface of the pastry with caster sugar. Fold in the long edges to meet in the centre. Dredge with caster sugar again and fold in half again lengthways. Press lightly with the rolling pin to seal the layers together.

Cut the pastry into slices about 0.5 cm (¼ inch) thick and place on a baking sheet. Open the centres out slightly to make a fan shape.

Bake in the oven at 220°C (425°F) mark 7 for 5–6 minutes until the pastry is well puffed and the sugar a light caramel colour. Turn the palmiers over and cook for a further 2–3 minutes until crisp and golden. Lift the pastries on to a wire rack and dust with sifted icing sugar before they are completely cold. Store in an airtight container.

Éclairs au Café

The pastry shapes can be made well in advance and kept in an airtight container, or even frozen, but once filled with cream they must be eaten within a few hours.

25 g (1 oz) butter
65 ml (2½ fl oz) water
30 g (1¼ oz) plain flour
1 egg, size 3, beaten
100 g (4 oz) icing sugar

10 ml (2 tsp) instant
  coffee
30 ml (2 tbsp) hot water
100 ml (4 fl oz) double
  cream

MAKES FIFTEEN

Sprinkle a baking sheet with water. Put the butter and water in a saucepan and bring to the boil. Sift the flour on to a sheet of greaseproof paper. When the butter mixture boils, remove the pan from the heat and tip in the flour all at once. Beat with a wooden spoon until the paste is smooth and comes away from the sides of the pan to form a ball in the centre. Allow to cool for 1–2 minutes.

Beat the egg into the paste, a little at a time, using a wooden spoon. Beat until smooth and shiny.

Spoon the mixture into a piping bag fitted with an 0.8 cm (⅜ inch) plain round nozzle. Pipe tiny éclairs about 2.5–4 cm (1–1½ inches) long on the prepared baking sheet, cutting the paste off cleanly with a wet knife for each one.

Bake in the oven at 200°C (400°F) mark 6 for 7 minutes until well risen. Increase the oven temperature to 220°C (425°F) mark 7 and bake for a further 5 minutes until crisp and golden.

Slit each éclair down the side with a sharp knife to allow the steam to escape, then return them to the oven for 1 minute to dry. Transfer to a wire rack.

Sift the icing sugar into a bowl. Dissolve the coffee in the hot water. Gradually stir the liquid coffee into the icing sugar until the icing is smooth and glossy and coats the back of a spoon. Spoon a little over the top of each cooled éclair.

Shortly before serving, whip the cream and pipe or spoon into the éclairs.

Coconut Thins

Lovely thin, crisp, tasty biscuits that keep surprisingly well in an airtight container.

25 g (1 oz) butter
25 g (1 oz) caster sugar
7.5 ml (½ tbsp) golden
  syrup
25 g (1 oz) plain flour

15 g (½ oz) desiccated
  coconut
5 ml (1 tsp) lemon juice

MAKES TWENTY

Oil two to three baking sheets. Cream the butter and sugar in a bowl until pale and fluffy. Beat in the golden syrup. Stir in the flour, desiccated coconut and lemon juice.

Take about 2.5 ml (½ tsp) of the mixture at a time, roll into a small ball and place on the prepared baking sheets, spacing them well apart.

Bake in the oven at 170°C (325°F) mark 3 for about 7 minutes until the edges are golden brown and the centres lightly coloured. Leave for a few moments on the baking sheets to harden. Lift them on to a wire rack, using a palette knife. When cold, store in an airtight container.

top ALMOND AND PISTACHIO FINGERS (page 85);
bottom LANGUES DE CHATS À L'ORANGE (page 81)

Petits Fours à la Génoise

A génoise mixture is always good for a cake you want to keep. These store well, becoming moister as the days go by.

75 g (3 oz) plain flour
pinch of salt
40 g (1½ oz) unsalted
  butter
3 eggs
75 g (3 oz) caster sugar
apricot glaze
350 g (12 oz) icing sugar
15–30 ml (1–2 tbsp) warm
  water

To decorate
crystallised violets
silver balls
nuts

MAKES FORTY

Lightly oil a 28×18 cm (11×7 inch) baking tin and line the base neatly with greaseproof paper. Oil the paper, then dust the paper and sides of the tin with flour.

Sift the flour twice with the salt and set aside. Warm the butter gently to melt, then leave to cool but do not let it solidify again. Break the eggs into a large bowl and gradually beat in the caster sugar with a hand held electric mixer. Place the bowl over a pan of hot water and whisk for about 10 minutes until the mixture is very thick, light and slightly warm.

Remove the bowl from the heat and continue whisking until the mixture cools and leaves a trail on itself. Resift the flour a little at a time on to the egg mixture and fold in lightly with a metal spoon. Add the melted butter, a little at a time, folding in carefully.

Pour the mixture into the prepared tin. Bake in the oven at 180°C (350°F) mark 4 for 25–30 minutes until the cake slightly shrinks away from the sides of the tin. The centre should spring back if lightly pressed with a finger. Leave to cool for a few minutes in the tin, then turn out on to a wire rack until completely cold.

When cold, use a serrated edged knife to cut the cake into small squares, about 2.5 cm (1 inch) each. Return them to the wire rack. Brush each one with a little warm apricot glaze.

Sift the icing sugar into a bowl and gradually stir in the warm water until the icing is smooth and glossy. Quickly spoon the icing over the little cakes and top with a variety of decorations, such as crystallised violets, silver balls, nuts.

Miniature Florentines

Deliciously crunchy, with a smooth chocolate backing, these are classic biscuits. Tiny ones make good petits fours.

15 g (½ oz) glacé cherries,
  roughly chopped
15 ml (1 tbsp) finely
  chopped candied peel
50 g (2 oz) chopped mixed
  nuts
25 g (1 oz) flaked almonds
40 g (1½ oz) butter

50 g (2 oz) caster sugar
15 ml (1 tbsp) double
  cream
100 g (4 oz) plain
  chocolate

MAKES TWENTY FIVE

Line two baking sheets with parchment. Put the cherries, candied peel and chopped and flaked nuts in a bowl. Melt the butter in a small saucepan, stir in the sugar and heat gently until dissolved. Bring to the boil and pour on to the fruit and nut mixture.

Add the cream and stir until thoroughly mixed in.

Using no more than 5 ml (1 level tsp) at a time, place little mounds of the mixture on the prepared baking sheets, spacing them well apart.

Bake in the oven at 180°C (350°F) mark 4 for 5 minutes. Remove from the oven and shape up each one into a neat round, using 5 cm (2 inch) pastry cutter. Return the biscuits to the oven for 3 minutes, then shape them again. Cook for a final 1 minute. If necessary, just tidy the edges again. Leave the biscuits on the baking sheets until they are just beginning to set, then lift on to a wire rack to cool.

Break the chocolate into a small bowl and melt it over a pan of hot water, stirring until smooth. Remove the pan from the heat, but leave the bowl over the hot water.

Using a small spreader, spread chocolate over the smooth side of each biscuit, then place them chocolate side up on the wire rack to set. Before the chocolate dries, mark in the traditional wavy lines, using an icing comb or fork.

Miniature Brandy Snaps

Brandy snaps can be eaten plain or filled with whipped cream, but cream should not be added until shortly before serving, as it will soften them.

25 g (1 oz) butter	25 g (1 oz) plain flour
25 g (1 oz) demerara sugar	tiny pinch of salt
25 g (1 oz) golden syrup	1.25 ml (¼ tsp) ground
1.25 ml (¼ tsp) lemon	ginger
juice	
drop of vanilla essence	MAKES EIGHTEEN

Thoroughly oil a baking sheet. Put the butter, sugar and golden syrup in a small saucepan and heat gently until the butter has melted and the sugar dissolved. Leave to cool slightly. Add the lemon juice and vanilla essence, then sift in the flour, salt and ground ginger. Stir until thoroughly mixed.

Spoon the mixture, 2.5 ml (½ tsp) (no more) at a time, on to the prepared baking sheet, spacing each spoonful about 7.5 cm (3 inches) apart. Leave the remaining mixture in the saucepan.

Bake in the oven at 170°C (325°F) mark 3 for 5–6 minutes. Leave to cool on the baking sheet for 1–2 minutes. Working quickly, lift each one in turn off the baking sheet with a palette knife and wrap it, flat side inwards, round the handle of a small wooden spoon. Leave for a few moments to harden then slide the brandy snap off and place on a wire rack. If the biscuits on the baking sheet harden too much, put them back in the oven for a few seconds.

Clean and oil the baking sheet, then repeat the process until all the mixture is used up. Do not bake two sheets at once, it makes the job too hectic when shaping. When cold, store in an airtight container.

Brandied Shortbread

Those who prefer something plain after dinner will love this. It is moist but still short.

175 g (6 oz) plain flour	few drops of brandy
75 g (3 oz) fine semolina	essence
175 g (6 oz) unsalted	20 g (¾ oz) blanched
butter	almonds
90 g (3½ oz) caster sugar	
15 ml (1 tbsp) brandy	MAKES TWENTY FOUR

Sift the flour and semolina together. Cream the butter, 75 g (3 oz) of the sugar, the brandy and essence together in a bowl. Mix in the flours to give a fairly sticky paste.

Spoon the paste into an 18 cm (7 inch) square shallow tin and mark into fingers. Split the blanched almonds along the natural break and scatter them over the top. Sprinkle with the remaining sugar.

Bake in the oven at 190°C (375°F) mark 5 for 15–20 minutes or until just set and a very pale golden colour. Leave to cool in the tin. Turn the shortbread out and break into slices along the marks. Store in an airtight container.

Spiced Sugared Almonds

These sugared almonds are crisp, not hard like the bought variety. If you prefer, the cinnamon may be omitted.

50 g (2 oz) blanched	1.25 ml (¼ tsp) ground
almonds	cinnamon
225 g (8 oz) basic fondant	orange food colouring
(see page 42)	
syrup stock (see page 42)	MAKES FIFTY

Spread the almonds on a baking sheet and lightly toast under grill or in the oven at 180°C (350°F) mark 4 for about 10 minutes. Leave to cool.

Melt the fondant in a bowl over hot water (see page 44), avoiding overheating. Add a little syrup stock if necessary to achieve a coating consistency. Add the cinnamon and tint the fondant a pale orange colour.

Using a dipping ring, dip the almonds, one at a time, into the fondant. Place on parchment to dry.

GLACÉ FRUIT (page 94)

Candied Fruits

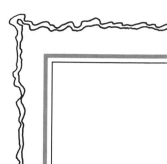

SUGAR, in high concentrations, is a marvellous preservative. Candying is a method of steeping fruit in sugar to such an extent that the natural deterioration of the fruit is slowed almost to a halt. As a bonus, it results in a highly luxurious confection. There are few people who could fail to be delighted with a gift of home-made candied fruits.

The process works by gradually increasing the concentration of sugar within the fruit. This has to be done slowly – an initial dipping would simply result in the sugar coating the outside of the fruit. By successive applications of heat, by gradually increasing the density of the syrup and by long periods of soaking, the sugar is persuaded to penetrate every fibre of the fruit.

Candied Fruit

This technique takes at least 16 days, demanding just a small amount of attention each day. No wonder candied fruits are so expensive to buy! The results, however, are well worth the trouble.

| fresh fruit, such as oranges, apricots, pineapple, kiwi, pears, apples | granulated sugar 30 ml (2 tbsp) orange flower water |

Day 1
Choose firm, ripe fruits, free from blemishes. Small fruits can be left whole but if they have tough skins

– such as plums or apricots – prick them all over with a fork; or halve them and remove the stones if you prefer. Remove the stones from cherries with a cherry stoner. Remove the peel from citrus fruits and divide oranges into segments, removing all pith and membrane. Peel pears, apples and peaches and halve them or cut into thick slices. Go over pineapple carefully to remove all the skin, core and 'eyes'; you can either cut the pineapple flesh into chunks or rings.

Weigh the fruit after preparation but before cooking. Always candy different types of fruit separately, so that they retain their individual flavours.

Put the prepared fruit in a saucepan, just cover with boiling water and simmer gently until just tender. Take care not to overcook the fruit, as soft fruits will have less taste and will loose their shape. On the other hand, if you undercook the fruit the finished product will be tough.

For every 450 g (1 lb) prepared fruit, use 175 g (6 oz) sugar and 300 ml (½ pint) of the water the fruit was cooked in.

Lift out the fruit carefully from the cooking liquid with a slotted spoon and place it in a large bowl. Do not heap the fruit up to much or the pieces at the bottom will get squashed – try to choose a wide bowl so that the fruit does not lie too deep.

Dissolve the sugar very slowly in the water, stirring continuously with a metal spoon. Bring to the boil and pour the syrup over the fruit. The fruit must be completely covered with syrup; if it isn't, make up more syrup of the same strength, but remember to increase the amount of sugar used on subsequent days in the same proportion. Leave to soak for a full 24 hours.

Day 2

Drain off the syrup into a saucepan and add another 50 g (2 oz) sugar. Dissolve it slowly over gentle heat, stirring continuously. Bring to the boil and pour the syrup back over the fruit. Soak for another 24 hours.

Days 3–7

Repeat that step every day for the next five days, so that the syrup gradually gets stronger and stronger.

Days 8–9

At the beginning of the second week, drain off the syrup and add 75 g (3 oz) sugar (instead of the 50 g (2 oz) you have been adding up to now). Dissolve it and then add the fruit to the syrup in the pan; simmer gently for 3–4 minutes. Carefully return the fruit and syrup to the bowl. Leave to soak for a full 48 hours.

Day 10

Repeat the same procedure with 75 g (3 oz) sugar. Then add 30 ml (2 tbsp) orange flower water and leave to soak for four full days. This is the last soaking and you can leave it longer if you wish, up to about two weeks; the fruit becomes sweeter and sweeter, the longer it is left.

Finally, drain off the syrup and spread the pieces of fruit out on a wire rack. Place the rack on a tray and cover the fruit without touching it, use an inverted roasting tin, a loose tent of foil, a plastic box – just to protect it from dust, flies etc. Leave the fruit in a warm place such as the airing cupboard or a warm corner of the kitchen until thoroughly dry – about two to three days. Turn each piece two or three times while drying.

When completely dry, carefully pack the candied fruits in boxes with waxed paper or parchment between each layer.

Glacé Fruit

The glacé process adds a crisp, glossy coating of sugar to the original preserved fruit.

---

candied fruit (see
  page 92)
450 g (1 lb) granulated
  sugar

150 ml (¼ pint) water

The candied fruit must be thoroughly dry. Put the sugar and water in a saucepan and dissolve the sugar slowly over a gentle heat, stirring. Bring to the boil and boil for about 1 minute.

Pour a little of the syrup into a small bowl and keep the rest warm over hot water. Put a little boiling water in another bowl.

Using a dipping fork or skewer, dip the candied fruit, one piece at a time, into the boiling water for about 20 seconds, then into the syrup. Place on a wire rack to dry. Replace the boiling water as it cools, and the syrup as it becomes cloudy. Dry the fruit again for two to three days, turning occasionally.

Index

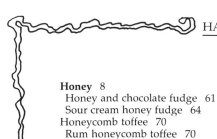